VICTORY IS YOURS

JONATHAN EVANS

HARVEST HOUSE PUBLISHERS
EUGENE, OREGON

Bible version copyright notifications are located at the back of the book.

Any emphasis within a Scripture quote is the author's.

Cover design by Faceout Studio

Cover images © subbery / Shutterstock

Interior design by KUHN Design Group

For bulk, special sales, or ministry purchases, please call 1-800-547-8979.
Email: CustomerService@hhpbooks.com

This logo is a federally registered trademark of the Hawkins Children's LLC. Harvest House Publishers, Inc., is the exclusive licensee of this trademark.

Special thanks to Kris Bearss for her collaboration on the development and content of this book.

Victory Is Yours

Published by Harvest House Publishers
Eugene, Oregon 97408
www.harvesthousepublishers.com

ISBN 978-0-7369-8696-0 (Hardcover)
ISBN 978-0-7369-8697-7 (eBook)

Library of Congress Control Number: 2024931184

Printed in the United States of America

25 26 27 28 29 30 31 32 / VP / 10 9 8 7 6 5 4 3 2 1

FOREWORD

by Dr. Tony Evans

It fills my heart with immense joy and pride to write this foreword for my son Jonathan's new devotional book, *Victory Is Yours*. As his father and mentor, I have been blessed to witness firsthand his growth, dedication, and unwavering commitment to inspiring others in their battle for victory. Through the pages of this devotional, he has captured the essence of the faith journey—sharing some of his own battles too—and provided a powerful resource for anyone seeking encouragement, biblical wisdom, and spiritual empowerment.

From the moment Jonathan embraced his calling to ministry, it became evident that God had bestowed on him a unique gift for connecting and communicating with people from all walks of life. Jonathan's empathy and passion for others shines through each thoughtfully crafted reading, speaking directly to the heart, addressing the deep concerns and fears that trouble believers, while also alerting us to many of the forces attempting to sabotage our faith. As Jonathan effectively illuminates the trials and the challenges we all face, he assures us of the important truth that victory is not only attainable but *already* attained through Jesus Christ. In a world filled with uncertainties and battles of every kind, this means victory is more than a distant dream; it is a present reality for those who are on the Lord's side.

I am confident that *Victory Is Yours* will reach far and wide, igniting a flame of hope and courage in your heart. You'll be urged to press on and guided to walk boldly in the path God has set before you. Jonathan's authenticity, unwavering faith, and commitment to walking in God's truth have been an inspiration to me and to all who have the privilege of knowing him personally. I pray that in the midst of *your* battles, the words you're about to read will be a guiding light and a source of inspiration and strength for you too.

May this devotional help each of us to remember that our heavenly Father longs to see us claim the victory Christ has already won on our behalf. And to my beloved son, congratulations on the publication of this compelling work. May God continue to use you mightily as a vessel of His grace and an instrument of His love.

INTRODUCTION:

BREAKTHROUGH!

I know of a guy who encountered an unexpected challenge while renovating an old home. After putting in several hours to remove the layers of plaster on one particularly stubborn wall, he was surprised to find a thick stone wall behind it. Wanting to adhere to his limited budget, he worked and worked at this obstacle over several days with the tools he had. It was taking a lot longer than he'd hoped, and he grew frustrated.

A few days later, he came back to the task with some heavy-duty professional tools he'd rented. In just a matter of minutes—*breakthrough!* But not because of the equipment. It turns out he had stopped just one thin layer from success. If only he had known how close he was to breaking through the wall, he would've kept going, determined and confident.

Spiritually, you never know how close you are to breaking through to the victory Jesus has already won for you. But if, in your fatigue, you're willing to have faith and carry out what God is calling you to do, He has the breakthrough ready.

That's the kind of encouragement we need. The encouragement to keep fighting for the win God promised and delivered on long ago. And it's what I've sought to give you through this devotional. We'll explore many of the challenges life in this world presents to us as men and women of faith. Everything from opposition and enemy attacks to times of waiting or loss, the struggles of our flesh, storms of doubt, and the difficulties of dealing with others.

Thanks to God, we never have to push through on our own strength. The Lord loves to show up strong for His sons and daughters. He loves to power our faith with reminders of His truth, His sufficiency, His faithfulness, His forgiveness, and His affection. As our Champion, He has already *saved* us. Now He stands ready to lead the way through our battles and *supply* us with what we need to persevere and follow Him all the way to victory.

Before God delivered him, the apostle Paul said in Philippians 1:18-19 that he *knew* God would deliver him. Our victory is about knowing. It's about what's absolute and true. It's about what God says through His Spirit and His Word, not what your battle is saying to you.

The truth is, in Him you're a conqueror, an overcomer. He's pronounced you the victor. You have His fighting Spirit within you. So no matter what you might be up against right now, that battle in your life is His to fight. And because of Him, the victory is yours.

You're almost there, believer. You may not think so yet, but your breakthrough is near. Read on, and don't give up!

1

A GOOD OUTLOOK

The LORD's acts of mercy indeed do not end, for His compassions do not fail. They are new every morning; great is Your faithfulness.

LAMENTATIONS 3:22-23

My wife and I have five kids ranging in age from preschool to high school, and on some mornings in our household, one or more of our children will wake up grumpy from the get-go. In those times, I have to remind them, "This is the day the LORD has made" (Psalm 118:24 NLT).

When you opened your eyes this morning, what was *your* outlook? Make no mistake, controlling your outlook is a sure way to make victory yours in both the everyday *and* in life's battles.

Lamentations 3:23 reminds us of how frequently God renews His mercies toward us: Every. Single. Morning. He makes them fresh each day. And He doesn't just dole them out one at a time. The plural nouns back this up: His "acts" of mercy are endless; His "compassions" never cease. The question we each have to answer is, *Am I living as if all of that applies to me right now, in the situation I'm feeling overwhelmed by?* Just as importantly, *Am I actively looking for His multiplied mercies?*

I know from my own life that if my countenance is down in the morning, it doesn't take much for my day to go down too. By the time we're at work or have dropped off the kids at school, we're complaining about every little thing. By lunchtime, we're sure the whole world is against us. By dinnertime, we're convinced that life won't ever go our way. And by bedtime, we're telling ourselves that even God isn't in our corner.

Let's stay out of that downward spiral and instead pray along with the psalmist for a fresh outlook: "Examine me, Lord… Refine my mind and my heart. For Your goodness is before my eyes" (Psalm 26:2-3).

Think About It: Keep a running list of God's goodness in your life so you can easily see all you may be overlooking in bad times.

2

ROUNDABOUT

I am teaching you the way of wisdom;
I am guiding you on straight paths.
When you walk, your steps will not be hindered;
when you run, you will not stumble.

PROVERBS 4:11-12 HCSB

We learned in geometry class that the shortest distance between two points is a straight line. So when I read here in Proverbs 4 that God guides me on straight paths if I look to Him, I'm good with that! I mean, who doesn't like a straight path? It's simpler. Direct. Faster.

Why, then, does He sometimes send us on winding detours? We find one reason in Exodus 13.

When the Israelites left Egypt, God didn't lead them along the main road that runs through Philistine territory, even though that was the shortest route to the promised land. He knew that if they faced enemy attack so early on, which was almost guaranteed on the direct route, they would choose to return to the "safety" of slavery in Egypt and never reach the territory He had reserved for them. "So God led them," says verse 18, "in a roundabout way through the wilderness toward the Red Sea" (NLT).

The street roundabouts, or traffic circles, that more and more cities are installing at extra-busy intersections can be similarly confusing and frustrating. They drive most of us crazy because we haven't mastered the art of going with the (traffic) flow. In response, we either speed through them dangerously, wanting to get past all the other drivers and out of the loop as fast as we can…or we move erratically, unsure.

But here's something to keep in mind. According to highway safety studies, roundabouts are hugely effective when navigated properly, reducing traffic fatalities and injuries by enormous margins. They're there for better and safer traffic flow.

The same could be said of God's roundabouts too.

So while you may be wondering, *Lord, what are You doing? Where's* my *straight path in all of this?* be sure that, for those who are following Him, His detours are as direct as He has determined they need to be. Don't fight Him. Don't get reckless. Don't pull back in fear. Take His route. He will get you where He's guiding you, and you'll get there right on time.

Think About It: God is the great Navigator for your life. He knows detours are necessary. Going straight sometimes leads to roadblocks. Trust Him anyway.

3

FEAR LESS

The LORD is for me;
I will not fear; what can man do to me?

PSALM 118:6

One of the realities I've noticed in the story of David and Goliath (1 Samuel 17) is this: Goliath knew exactly how to disintegrate the courage of his opponents. Stepping out from the Philistine ranks, he "came forward morning and evening, and took his stand," shouting threats at the army of Israel and defying their God (verse 16). Instead of rising up in righteous anger, strong and courageous, an entire nation of warriors—including their king—shrank back, "dismayed and very fearful" (verse 11).

Israel's fear apparently didn't subside either. Instead, it got worse. Goliath's daily routine went on for nearly six weeks, and after a while, even though his opponents knew exactly what he would say, the Philistine no longer had to say a word. The army of Israel would run away at just the sight of him.

That's a picture of the fear of man overtaking the fear of God. Yet even a quick review of the Lord's "résumé and qualifications" could have moved these men to action against Goliath. Moses had this to say about Israel's God, who had drowned Pharaoh's army in the Red Sea:

> The LORD is a warrior; the LORD is His name… Your right hand, LORD, is majestic in power; Your right hand, LORD, destroys the enemy. And in the greatness of Your excellence You overthrow those who rise up against You (Exodus 15:3, 6-7).

I realize it's not easy to stand fearless when someone or something so seemingly powerful is threatening us. But let's start with fearing *less*—"because He who is in you is greater than he who is in the world" (1 John 4:4 NKJV). It might involve remembering your own history with God. Or opening God's "autobiography," the Bible, and reading up on His past exploits. Just know that, with this Warrior, history *does* repeat itself. He is as able as ever to overthrow anyone who stands against Him and His people. Call on Him for your deliverance. The Lord is His name.

Think About It: Thanks to God, His people never have to fight *for* victory. We are always fighting *from* victory.

4

THE CONSTANT FIGHT

Faith is confidence in what we hope for
and assurance about what we do not see.

HEBREWS 11:1 NIV

The constant fight between faith and sight is ingrained in us as human beings.

From the early days of Eden, God said, "Live My way in faith and you will never lack anything. You'll have life and abundance and be at peace with each other and with Me. Just don't eat the fruit of this one tree." Well, we're all living with the consequences of what Adam and Eve did with that choice. Instead of obeying the Lord, they took a different course of action. One that looked good and seemed pleasant *to them* (Genesis 3:6). And their choice ended in destruction.

In yet another biblical scene (Numbers 13–14), though God had promised to give the land of Canaan to the people of Israel, 10 of the 12 spies Moses sent out to surveil the territory were a "no-go" once they saw the people who lived there. Sure, the land was bountiful and would be a great place to live, they said. "It certainly does flow with milk and honey," they said. "Nevertheless, the people who live in the land are strong, and the cities are fortified and very large…We are not able to go up against the people, because they are too strong for us" (13:27-28, 31). This bad report made the Israelites want to stone Moses and head back to Egypt rather than inhabit their inheritance. As for those ten men? They lost out on the opportunity to live in the promised land.

Here's one more instance. The disciples were on the sea in a really bad storm. They saw Jesus walking on the waves toward them, and He told them, "Take heart; it is I. Do not be afraid" (Matthew 14:27 ESV). At Jesus's invitation, Peter got out of the boat and started walking on water too. That is, until "he saw the wind" (verse 30 ESV). Then he grew afraid and began to sink.

Numerous times in Scripture, those who acted on the "certainty" of their physical eyes experienced less than what could have been had they entrusted themselves to the Lord. The same can be said of us if we are making our decisions only on *things seen*. Seek God's will and His Word first and most, no matter what is in front of you. His greatest blessings lie beyond your sight.

Think About It: Just because you see a way doesn't mean you're seeing God's way. His vision for your life is much greater than what lies within your line of vision.

5

WISH LIST

A man's heart plans his way,
but the L*ORD* *determines his steps.*

PROVERBS 16:9 HCSB

What's on your list? You have one, right? Maybe it's not written down. Maybe it's in the form of a vision board or a ten-year plan. Doesn't matter, it still counts.

So which ones are yours? A bucket list of things you'd like to do before you die? Your must-haves for your future mate? That spreadsheet of current projects at work or your portfolio of investments? A calendar showing your kid's extracurricular activities? Your wedding registry, the colleges you're considering, or the neighborhoods you've favorited as potential places to live? I keep two lists: future vacation spots and ideas for quality time with my wife.

God is all in favor of planning ahead. Entire chapters in Exodus relay His instructions to Moses for building the tabernacle. Proverbs 21:5 lauds good planning and diligence as keys to success, and Luke 14 says that wise people count the costs before proceeding with a venture. There's real value in having dreams and goals. Let's just make sure that as you and I are planning and prioritizing, we're running everything by the Lord first.

Some people think it's silly to pray over anything except the big stuff. "Nobody asks God about their wedding registry or investments," they say. But I know for a fact that people are praying over these exact things. Why not you?

Pastor Dwight L. Moody once said that while most people do believe in God, "what they will not do is give Him exclusive right of way." Giving God first right-of-refusal is letting Him reign in your life. Giving Him permission to edit you is seeking the mind of Christ about the things that are on your mind.

God cares about everything you care about. If it's on your mind, it's on His. So ask Him what He thinks, and be willing to adjust your plans accordingly. When you "commit to the Lord whatever you do…he will establish your plans" (Proverbs 16:3 NIV).

Think About It: If a father cares about his children enough to listen to the little things, how much more does our heavenly Father care about all that's on our hearts? Talk to Him. He wants to process plans with you.

6

CAN'T? OR WON'T?

You were taught, with regard to your former way of life, to put off your old self, which is being corrupted by its deceitful desires; to be made new in the attitude of your minds; and to put on the new self, created to be like God in true righteousness and holiness.

EPHESIANS 4:22-24 NIV

In his book *Come Before Winter*, Pastor Charles Swindoll talks about the difference between *can't* and *won't* in the Christian life. "Any Christian who takes the Scriptures seriously will have to confess the word [*can't*] really should be *won't*. Why? Because we have been given the power, the ability to overcome!"[1]

That's a huge difference between Christians and non-Christians. Paul's description in Ephesians 4:17-18 was that the unsaved "live...in the futility of their thinking...darkened in their understanding and separated from the life of God because of the ignorance that is in them due to the hardening of their hearts" (NIV). He said in Romans 8:7 that the mind set on the flesh does not submit to God and "indeed, it cannot," adding in verse 8, "Those who are in the flesh cannot please God" (ESV). Swindoll summarizes, "Non-Christians have every right and reason to use *can't*, because they really can't...Without Christ and His power, they lack what it takes to change permanently."[2] For Christians, however, it's a different story. "We don't because we won't...we disobey because we want to, not because we have to...because we choose to, not because we're forced to."[3]

The words of Romans 6:6 deliver some powerfully good news for any believer who wants to reverse course: You *can.* "Our old self was crucified with [Christ], in order that our body of sin might be done away with, so that we would no longer be slaves to sin." Paul added in Colossians 3:8, "Rid yourselves of all of them: anger, wrath, malice, slander, and obscene speech."

We can do this now. We can rid ourselves of the dark, dead thoughts or deeds that Satan once buried us under. After all, we are no longer dead men or women walking. We are alive in Christ, resurrected by love, compelled to holiness by the One who called us, inhabited by the Spirit of God.

Christ's redemption and resurrection has freed us completely, clearing the path for a life of righteousness, lasting change, and victory. Praise God, you and I can leave both *can't* and *won't* in the dust, now and forever.

Think About It: You were traded to a new team with a new uniform and called to operate from a new Playbook. The old team is no longer calling the shots. It's time to submit to your new Coach.

7

BUILD!

Noah was a righteous man,
blameless among the people of his time,
and he walked faithfully with God.

GENESIS 6:9 NIV

Everybody knows that Noah built an ark, but did you ever think about the environment he was building in? God called him to build in an environment that was apparently even worse than ours. The Nephilim were on the earth. These were demonized men who were having sexual relations with women, and these women gave birth to an evil race. So the men of earth were absent, or at least not doing what they were supposed to do. The people of earth were wicked and violent. And their hearts were so dark, Genesis 6 reports that "every inclination" they had "was only evil all the time" and that "the LORD regretted" ever creating human beings (verses 5-6 NIV).

Despite this evil, unsupportive environment, Noah was called to build a saving environment. You're called to build a saving environment too—and not simply when you have support.

Some of you are reading this and talking at me right now, saying, "Man, I have generational curses. If you knew my family, you'd know why things in my life have fallen apart. We're in disarray...I only wish my family was more like yours."

Okay, bro. Okay, sis. Don't just wish. Pray! You can wish for a million things, but prayer activates a million things. Then get to work. Pick up the hammer and nails and pound away every day until your ark is built.

God is calling you to be the one to break the curse. Noah was building for more than a hundred years, totally by faith. I want you to think about that. Focus on building. Even if you haven't had that family support, even if you feel like you're the only one fighting for change, understand that Noah and his family found favor with the Lord despite the disarray in the marriages and families in that culture.

At God's command, Noah built something that saved his family. Are you building a structure, an environment, to save your family? Are you building to give your family, your marriage, your children (or your future marriage and children) a safe place to get on board? Stay faithful and focused, no matter how long it takes. Noah's God is your God. Keep building.

Think About It: Your family's history may be a mess, but what are you doing to upend the mess? What are you building to reverse the curse? Make this a priority in prayer.

8

BIBLICAL BUILDING CODES

You are...members of [God's] household, built on the foundation of the apostles and prophets, with Christ Jesus himself as the chief cornerstone. In him the whole building is joined together and rises to become a holy temple in the Lord.

EPHESIANS 2:19-21 NIV

What are you aiming to build? Where in your life are you breaking ground?

These biblical "building codes" apply anytime you're starting something new. Whether you're getting married, launching a business, having a baby, or entering retirement and wanting to make the most of it, this is how you build that "new house" in the Lord's name.

First, *make Christ your cornerstone*. Those who trust in Him as the "cornerstone, a sure foundation" for their plans, relationships, and decisions will be "unshakable" (Isaiah 28:16 HCSB).

Second, *follow God's blueprint*. The teachings of the Bible aren't just there for decoration or feel-good inspiration. We *stand* on the Word of God. We frame our entire lives around it. Therefore, we have to study it like the blueprint-for-life that it is. God's Word is that important.

Third, *install bright lights and good plumbing.* Jesus promised His followers would have "the Light of life" (John 8:12), and from their "innermost being" would "flow rivers of living water" (7:38). A major reason for building anything—a marriage, a home, a business—is to bless and refresh others through it and introduce them to the Lord: "Let your light shine before others, that they may see your good deeds and glorify your Father in heaven" (Matthew 5:16 NIV).

Fourth, *power the place with love.* We're commanded in 1 Corinthians 16:14, "Do everything in love" (NIV). God's love is the power supply for a life of faith and impact. The more you draw on Him in all you do, the more others will be drawn to connect to Him too.

Last but not least, *cover the entire dwelling in prayer.* Without exception, you're going to encounter rough weather during certain seasons in your marriage, your career, your parenting, and so on. God hears the prayers of those who live for Him (Psalm 66:19). The house built on faith from the ground up can withstand any climate or conditions.

Think About It: You never know if a structure was built correctly until a storm comes. When the storm hits, what will it reveal about your structure?

9

THE PRICE OF IMPATIENCE

Behold, the eye of the LORD is on those who fear Him,
on those who wait for His faithfulness.

PSALM 33:18

I don't know of anybody who likes to wait. Just the thought of being eighth on the sign-in list at the doctor's office or standing in that crazy-long line to renew a driver's license will test anyone's patience. What I've come to realize, though, is that anytime we give in to impatience, whether it's over something big or something small, our impatience comes at a price. Not just outbursts of anger or high blood pressure, but bad decisions.

Esau forfeited his inheritance because he was hungry. Saul lost his throne because he wouldn't wait just a little longer for Samuel to arrive and offer the sacrifice. And Aaron built the Israelites an idol to worship because they were worried that Moses was never returning from Mount Sinai (where, incidentally, God was giving him the Ten Commandments).

Impatience got the best of some of the biggest names in the Bible. You and I are no exception. I mean, haven't you tried to solve the wait or shorten the wait in some way?

It's human nature to want a quick solution—we'd rather sprint and get it over with than endure a marathon test of faith. We'd rather pop a pill for our symptoms than go through surgery and be healed. Expect this temptation so you won't be surprised when shortcuts and schemes come to mind. And prepare to resist, understanding that none of these ideas will get you through the wait any faster. If anything, working against God's timing will add to your troubles and possibly prolong them. There simply isn't any hope for real resolution if you and I turn aside for a solution that isn't His.

I like the standard that Samuel the prophet held up for the people of Israel—a standard he himself lived by: "Do not turn aside from following the LORD, but serve the LORD with all your heart. And do not turn aside after empty things [including those schemes circulating in your brain] that cannot profit or deliver…The LORD will not forsake his people" (1 Samuel 12:20-22 ESV).

Think About It: You will never get the best God has for you if you let your impatience get the best of you.

10

STEP UP

We are God's handiwork, created in Christ Jesus to do good works, which God prepared in advance for us to do.

EPHESIANS 2:10 NIV

I've heard many Christians make comments over the years suggesting they're "a nobody" who has nothing to contribute to the ministry of the church because...

"I can't sing or play an instrument."

"I'm too shy to get up in front of people and talk."

"I don't know the Bible like older Christians do."

"I've never been the leadership type."

While some people use those comments as an excuse to avoid getting involved, the ones I'm focused on here are those who really mean what they're saying. They honestly believe there's no way they can make a difference.

If that's you, friend, then the enemy has you right where he wants you—on the sidelines, sitting it out, convinced you either have no gifts, or your gifts are too small to matter. He and his troops are warring against Christ and His church, and as far as the devil is concerned, the fewer fighting on heaven's side, the better.

The thing is, Christ has already sent you onto the field. He sent all His disciples on a reconnaissance mission to locate and rescue the lost in His name. What's more, He has assigned *you* a specific position and a unique role that only you can fill within His church. If you're not sure about yours, read up on spiritual gifts or take a class at church—then take your position and do your part!

You have a sacred mission to carry out. God has appointed souls for you to pray over. He has feats of strength in the faith for you to accomplish. Tasks you've been created for and spiritually equipped to complete. Testimonies of Christ's power in your weakness that He intends for you to tell others. Don't make Jesus come looking for you. Step up and ask, "Where do You want me?"

With each prayer you pray, each encouraging word you speak, each hug you give, and each person you help, the forces of darkness take another hit. They forfeit another inch of ground. And the Lord's army adds another warrior, quickening the enemy's demise.

Think About It: You are not drafted by the grace of God to sit on the bench. You have been drafted to play the game. Let's go!

11

ON AUTHORITY

We did not follow cunningly devised fables
when we made known to you the power and coming
of our Lord Jesus Christ, but were eyewitnesses of His majesty.

2 PETER 1:16 NKJV

It really doesn't matter what we believe.

Now, before you close this book and call me names, hear me out. Put the emphasis on *we*. Then read that first sentence over again.

You see, lots of folks believe lots of things, but their belief doesn't determine what is true. For example, talk to enough people, and you'll meet at least a few who are sure the moon landing was a hoax. Others, despite photos from space, are convinced our planet is flat. And enough Americans believe in the existence of Sasquatch that Animal Planet's TV show *Finding Bigfoot* ran for 12 seasons. So when I say it doesn't matter what *we* believe, I'm saying we humans can be convinced of all sorts of things whether they're true or not. What does matter is that what we believe is *true*. Then what we believe matters beyond words.

Do you follow me? You can't just let what your mom or your buddy or some talking head says be the basis for your belief. Like those people, your belief is valid only if you're getting it from a completely reliable authority. And for matters of life and faith, the Bible is that authority.

Maybe you're skeptical or unsure about how reliable today's Bible is. Books like *The Unshakable Truth* by Josh and Sean McDowell or *I Don't Have Enough Faith to Be an Atheist* by Norman L. Geisler and Frank Turek will assure you with scholarly evidence from various fields of research.

The Bible isn't just some collection of ancient morality tales and wisdom sayings like many people believe. It records the acts of God in human history, along with His actual thoughts and words. Not only that, but it is the authoritative record of Christ's life. And the continuing discoveries of archaeologists and historians only further corroborate its reliability.

So the next time you read Jesus saying, "Truly I tell you, until heaven and earth disappear, not the smallest letter, not the least stroke of a pen, will by any means disappear from the Law until everything is accomplished" (Matthew 5:18 NIV)—believe it! You have it on the very best authority.

Think About It: You're pledging your allegiance to something. If the Bible is not your authority, then something else with much less authority is.

12

ON GUARD

Set a guard, Lord, over my mouth;
keep watch over the door of my lips.

PSALM 141:3

I remember one of the times I was reminded (once again) of the need to guard my words. Kanika's and my middle daughter, Kylar, had made her way into Mommy and Daddy's bed in the middle of the night, on a night when I was extra-tired. Without thinking, and half-asleep, I told her, "I'm tired, Kylar; I don't want you in the bed tonight."

At hearing that, our little girl started crying. "You don't want me, Daddy?"

Talk about regrets...I had broken her heart with my careless words, and you can bet I woke up fast to mend things between us.

Knowing that our words can leave not only wounds but also permanent scars, those of us who love Christ must be careful to set a guard over our mouths. Most of us are prone to saying things we regret when we're upset or running low physically. So when you know you're already under stress, or you're feeling hungry or tired, be extra-vigilant about guarding your tongue, and have the Holy Spirit keep watch with you.

Silence is often the best "answer," where you actually deadbolt the door of your lips. Proverbs 17:28 advises, "Even a fool who keeps silent is considered wise" (ESV). For those times when words are necessary, God calls for "a gentle answer" (Proverbs 15:1) and speech that is seasoned with grace (Colossians 4:6). Make no mistake—a gracious answer can still express a boundary or firmly correct someone. In fact, Ephesians 4:26 clearly states (and Jesus modeled) that you can be angry without sinning.

Ultimately, in the war over our words, there's almost no stopping the godly one who will not abandon their post.

Do you aspire to be an even greater force for good in this world and in your relationships? Then start here. Set a guard and keep watch over the door of your lips.

Think About It: According to Proverbs 21:23, "Whoever keeps his mouth and his tongue keeps himself out of trouble" (ESV). Silence at the right times makes your life simpler and safer.

13

SLOW DOWN

Be…slow to speak, and slow to anger; for a man's anger does not bring about the righteousness of God.

JAMES 1:19-20

We have to think before we speak. There's just no way around it. Otherwise, our words are like explosives set to detonate. One trip of our tongues, and everybody gets hurt.

Here are a few ideas to help us be more mindful and less impulsive in our responses:

First, *train yourself to slow down.* Proverbs 15:28 explains, "The heart of the righteous ponders how to answer, but the mouth of the wicked pours out evil things." *Pondering* is holding your tongue by the power of the Holy Spirit *until*: Until you've had a chance to back off from the heat of the moment and collect yourself. Until you can empathize and see the other person's point of view. And, in more volatile situations, until you've run your thoughts past a gut-honest friend or mentor who won't let you just put someone on blast.

Second, *focus on building your character.* James cautions about being "slow to anger" too. Real restraint and patience come from the inside, where the Holy Spirit does His deepest work. He makes setting aside defensiveness, your "rights," and pride more than possible for the sake of grace.

Third, *get to know your hot buttons*. What circumstances typically push your buttons—situations where you're quicker to let words fly? Those "idiot" drivers on the afternoon commute? Sunday mornings, when you're trying to get the entire household out the door to church? Maybe your uncle's political statements at family gatherings or your coworker's constant gossip?

Do more than identify those pressure points. Go a step further and examine why they bother you. Getting to the root can help you weed out harmful ways of thinking. And if your thoughts are being transformed, your reactions will change as well.

Finally, *strategize to counteract your hot buttons*. Challenge yourself to let three people in front of you during your drive home from work. Wake up 15 minutes earlier this Sunday to try to get ahead of the chaos. And in advance of those combative relatives or coworkers, rehearse a couple of statements that will respectfully let them know where you draw the line conversationally. Before you know it, the grace response might become more than an occasional thing. It might actually, miraculously, become second nature!

Think About It: Have you put strategy into working out your salvation? Without a spiritual strategy, you have very little chance for change.

14

THAT FIGHTING SPIRIT

You will receive power when the Holy Spirit has come upon you, and you will be my witnesses in Jerusalem and in all Judea and Samaria, and to the end of the earth.

ACTS 1:8 ESV

You college sports fans know that when the "Vols" come to town, your team will be playing the University of Tennessee Volunteers. But where did that unusual team name come from?

According to the website of the Tennessee Historical Society, Tennessee first became known as "the Volunteer State" thanks to the critical role its volunteer militia played in the War of 1812. The fighting spirit of its citizens was further demonstrated a few decades later during the Mexican American War, when President James K. Polk issued a call for 2,600 volunteers from his home state to join in the military effort...and 30,000 Tennesseans answered.

That amazing response from the people of Tennessee back then presents a worthy challenge for God's people now. Can you imagine how many spiritual battles would be won in this world if every citizen of God's kingdom would simply answer His call from wherever they were? Just by those men and women reporting for duty, workplaces would be changed. Families and marriages would be healed. Lives would be saved. And entire nations would be won for Christ.

There's no denying that the front lines are a place of serious business. Of the thousands of Tennesseans who answered the president's call, most of them probably had very real fears or concerns. Who wouldn't, leaving home and loved ones to do battle? Even with the first disciples whom Jesus called to "go…and make disciples of all the nations," the Gospel of Matthew reports "some were doubtful." I believe that's why Jesus couched His commission with two iron-clad statements: "All authority in heaven and on earth has been given to Me" on the front end, and "Behold, I am with you always, to the end of the age" on the back end (Matthew 28:16-20). His volunteers needed to know Christ's power and His presence would be theirs.

What was true then is still true. The battle is on. Christ has issued the call: "The harvest is plentiful, but the laborers are few" (Luke 10:2). Wherever you are, however you can…answer it. His Spirit is with you in the fight.

Think About It: Let's follow the example of Isaiah and how he volunteered—"I heard the voice of the Lord, saying, 'Whom shall I send, and who will go for Us?' Then I said, 'Here am I. Send me!'" (Isaiah 6:8).

15

CAPTIVATED

Having been justified by faith, we have peace with God through our Lord Jesus Christ, through whom we also have obtained our introduction by faith into this grace in which we stand; and we celebrate in hope of the glory of God.

ROMANS 5:1-2

Peace and intimacy with God are realities to be celebrated. Unfortunately, just like in New Testament times, some of the spiritual leaders in our world today are teaching a works-based righteousness, as if Jesus's work isn't enough. As if we can somehow earn our way to heaven by tithing or doing good deeds or praying longer and louder than anybody else. This is often accompanied by a theology that characterizes God as angry—just waiting for us to mess up so He can make us pay.

Let me be clear. First, Jesus paid *once and for all* for every sin of yours and every sin of mine...so that we don't have to. We are justified and saved by faith in Christ alone, not by anything we do. Second, His sacrifice was sufficient. Period. Third, a harsh, narrow view of God is one of Satan's schemes to keep people chained to fear. Feeling obligated to obey the Lord in hopes of reaching heaven, or to escape His wrath, is what we call legalism.

But Paul's wording in his New Testament letters was even clearer: *slavery*. Legalism makes people captive to rule-following and spiritual box-checking, when what really matters is growing more and more captivated with Christ and living close to Him.

God's plan to send His Son to earth and Christ's sacrifice on the cross had everything to do with love and nothing to do with legalism. Our Father in heaven not only released enslaved sinners from what bound them but welcomed them into His family as beloved sons and daughters. Each of these decisions was motivated by God's pure desire for a relationship with each of us.

"It was for freedom that Christ set us free," explains Paul to his readers in Galatians 5:1. "Therefore keep standing firm and do not be subject again to a yoke of slavery." Romans 8:1-2 proclaims, "There is now no condemnation for those who are in Christ Jesus, because through Christ Jesus the law of the Spirit who gives life has set you free from the law of sin and death" (NIV).

Jesus set us free to live in the victory of divine grace, not human works. Next time somebody tries to tell you differently, remind yourself of Jesus's own words: "If the Son sets you free, you will be free indeed" (John 8:36 ESV).

Think About It: A prisoner cannot set themselves free unless someone outside the jail uses the key. Jesus used the key. Now by grace, go live in victory.

16

A COORDINATED OFFENSE

I will instruct you and teach you in the way which you should go; I will advise you with My eye upon you.

PSALM 32:8

With every football team I ever played for, from high school through the NFL, our offensive plan always included a couple of stretch plays. This is where a running back is called on to use his speed to go *around* the defense instead of through the defense. One time, against the Chicago Bears, my teammates and I were able to execute the stretch play so well that our runner broke free for a 40-yard touchdown to win the game.

That sure was fun! A strong game plan and great coordination between coach and players produced a celebration that still puts a grin on my face all these years later. It's a picture of how we ought to be operating in our lives too. Following our divine Coach's plan and play calls is a winning strategy for our daily decisions as much as our battles on the field.

Spiritually, however, I can think of situations when I called my own stretch play, treating God like an opponent I was trying to escape. While I had good intentions to run around my problem, I was actually running around His will. And you can guess the outcome. All I did was pile on trouble. I got knocked out of bounds, tripped up by my own foolishness. Occasionally I initially picked up a few yards, but defeat and disappointment were waiting for me once I turned the corner. In reality, I wasn't contributing toward a coordinated offense. I was leaving myself isolated and vulnerable out there in the open field.

The only way to win in your life and your battles is to follow God's game plan. Look to Him for all of it: to make the call, choose the timing, set blockers in place, and guide each player's moves. Trust me, that's how you will score in your circumstances and ultimately how you'll experience the victory in your life.

Think About It: God has given you this word—"I know the plans I have for you…plans to prosper you and not to harm you, plans to give you hope and a future" (Jeremiah 29:11 NIV). Run His play!

17

STUBBORN FAITH

Resist [your adversary, the devil], firm in your faith.

1 PETER 5:9

Dog lovers know how hard man's best friend will latch onto a bone. My favorite dog was a pit bull named Blue who was built like a tank. Let me tell you, though I was a Division I college football player in peak physical condition, I would've had a tough time getting a bone out of Blue's mouth once he had his jaws around it. Such a big, full-grown dog was just too strong and too stubborn to let go of a good thing.

You and I should strive to be just that stubborn when it comes to holding fast to our faith. No matter how strong the enemy is, our faith should prove to be stronger when he tries to steal it from us.

The Bible warns us that Satan is hungry and on the prowl (1 Peter 5:8). Anytime the devil shows up in the yard of your faith, you can guarantee he's not there to sit and watch you play around. He's there for one purpose: "to steal and kill and destroy" (John 10:10). He may come at your faith by stealth, or forcefully to your face, but he has his eye on you and what is yours through faith in Christ.

Will you stubbornly trust the Lord and His promises in the face of cancer or job loss or infertility? In the face of injustice or depression or a relationship breakup? Will you resolve to say, amid your sorrow or confusion or anger, "I believe that I shall look upon the goodness of the LORD in the land of the living" (Psalm 27:13 ESV)?

By the blood of Christ, the truth of God's Word, and the power of the Holy Spirit, you can—and will. Stay stubborn, believer, and do not let go!

Think About It: The enemy has already lost, and you have already won. So seize your victory.

18

THE HARVEST AHEAD

Let's not get tired of doing what is good.
At just the right time we will reap a harvest
of blessing if we don't give up.

GALATIANS 6:9 NLT

If we must do battle as Christians, who wouldn't prefer the weeklong Battle of Jericho versus something that goes on for years? The ones that stretch us to our limits are the ones we have to persevere in. Like caring for a loved one with a terminal illness. Struggles with clinical depression, chronic pain, addiction, or anxiety. Loving a prodigal son or daughter. Or honoring your vows in a difficult marriage.

In today's verse, we see how Paul encouraged fellow sufferers. It's tempting to read his words and say, "Easier said than done, Paul." Except he was a guy who "done" what he said.

While being falsely accused and unjustly held in jail for more than two years, he wrote letter after letter to the churches he oversaw. He also actively shared the gospel with other prisoners and his guards. I could name many saints in my own life who, by God's grace, have found impactful ways to minister from the middle of their difficulty, like Paul did. That getting-outside-of-themselves focus helped get them through. And I believe it's because they were counting on God's promise of a coming harvest.

They understood there's no such thing as killing time when you're on God's time. This coincides with Hebrews 10:24-25, where the redeemed of the Lord are advised, "Let's consider how to encourage one another in love and good deeds...and *all the more* as you see the day drawing near."

How about you? What good will you purposely do today, knowing your labor is not in vain? No matter what, don't grow passive! Keep cultivating. Plant seeds, pull weeds, irrigate the soil—take care of whatever God is asking of you during this growing season. You're waiting on the Lord of the harvest. And it won't be long.

Think About It: Everyone wants a harvest and the feast that follows, but are you willing to persevere in the plowing and planting?

19

WHO'S THE GREATEST?

Be imitators of God, as beloved children; and walk in love, just as Christ also loved you and gave Himself up for us, an offering and a sacrifice to God as a fragrant aroma.

EPHESIANS 5:1-2

Remember the early '90s television commercial "Be Like Mike"? I do. Gatorade's famous advertising spot featured legendary NBA player Michael Jordan and catchy music that had millions of people singing, "I want to be like Mike."

Even today, a full 20 years after Jordan's retirement from the pros, basketball players still want to be like the 14-time NBA All-Star who led his teams to six league championships. In fact, in an anonymous 2023 *Sports Illustrated* poll, almost 60 percent of *current* NBA players named the ten-time scoring leader and record-setting defender the GOAT, the Greatest of All Time.

Jordan set the bar incredibly high as a sports champion. Christ the LAMB (John 1:29), however, has called kingdom champions much higher. He has called them to be like Him—by humbling themselves.

Jesus specified the path to greatness when two of His disciples started arguing about which one of *them* was the greatest:

"The one who is the greatest among you," He said, "must become like the youngest [a child], and the leader like the servant." And in case there was any question about who exemplified this, their Savior said, "I am among you as the one who serves" (Luke 22:26-27).

The sad irony is that this conversation happened during the Last Supper. Just after Jesus had washed their feet and led His men in communion, telling them, "This [bread] is my body given for you...This cup is the new covenant in my blood, which is poured out for you" (Luke 22:19-20 NIV). Imagine posturing in front of the one and only Lamb of God on the night before He would voluntarily give up His *life* to serve as the all-time sacrifice for sin!

Do you want to be a champion for the Lord? John the Baptist had it right when he said of himself in comparison to Christ: "He must become greater; I must become less" (John 3:30 NIV). Stop elbowing for the top spot and choose a life of humble sacrifice like Jesus, who "did not come to be served, but to serve" (Mark 10:45).

Think About It: In the kingdom of God, the lowly Servant is our highest standard.

20

SECURITY CLEARANCE

If any of you lacks wisdom, he should ask God,
who gives to all generously and without criticizing,
and it will be given to him.

JAMES 1:5 HCSB

Not every enlistee in the US military gets security clearance. It depends on a person's duties, the type of information they need to access—and most of all, whether their conduct and character pass the layers of scrutiny required for confidential, secret, or top-secret classification.

This makes me thankful that the Commander of heaven's army operates differently. There's no bureaucracy involved. No months of paperwork, interviews, and background checks. *And*... no suspicion or condemnation for wanting more understanding of the truths of the kingdom. Anytime you or I lack wisdom, God freely and generously gives access if we simply ask. What's more, we are granted the double blessing of both clarity and protection in our missions with Him.

I can't say it better than Solomon did in Proverbs 2, so I'll let him communicate the remarkable advantages of having access to the wisdom of heaven.

> You will understand the fear of the LORD and find the knowledge of God. For the LORD gives wisdom; from his mouth come knowledge and understanding. He holds success in store for the upright, he is a shield to those whose walk is blameless, for he guards the course of the just and protects the way of his faithful ones. Then you will understand what is right and just and fair—every good path. For wisdom will enter your heart, and knowledge will be pleasant to your soul. Discretion will protect you, and understanding will guard you (verses 5-11 NIV).

This is only the beginning. The benefits of wisdom don't end here. But at least now you know to ask—and to ask unafraid. God's answer will always be, "Permission granted." And your personnel file has already been stamped "Access granted," now and forever.

Think About It: The 31 chapters in the book of Proverbs speak of dozens of advantages of wisdom. To start accessing the secrets of God, plan sometime soon to read a chapter a day for a month.

21

BECAUSE YOU SAY SO

We have come to share in Christ, if indeed we hold our original confidence firm to the end. As it is said, "Today, if you hear his voice, do not harden your hearts."

HEBREWS 3:14-15 ESV

It had been "one of those days" on the job for Simon Peter and his fishing partners, the brothers James and John. A frustrating, tiring day when their best efforts had yielded zero results. And now this teacher known as Jesus was sitting in Simon's fishing boat, telling him to head for deep water to let down his nets for a catch.

At first, my man responded, "Master...we've worked hard all night long and caught nothing!" Putting in the overtime with no reward had worn him out, and it's very possible he was thinking what any of us would think: *Are You really asking me this right now?* I don't know if Jesus gave Simon one of those looks, or if Simon was more trusting than I would be, but his next statement was the key: "But at Your word, I'll let down the nets" (Luke 5:5 HCSB). The NIV Bible translates it, "But because you say so..."

Although exhausted, Peter consented to go back out and

cast his nets. Although discouraged, he put his trust in the One who called him.

Soon, his boat was so loaded down with fish, he had to call on the bros to bring their boat too, and the same thing happened with them: They could barely stay afloat due to the abundance of the catch. Then, to cap off their dream day on the water, all three men accepted Christ's invitation to follow Him and become fishers of men. (Luke 5:1-11 tells the whole story.)

I guarantee you, as soon as those fish started jumping into the nets, Peter had fresh energy. More importantly, on that day on the Sea of Galilee, Jesus cast a vision for His disciple that kept Peter going through all the ups and downs of ministry for the rest of his life.

You may be at a low point yourself, ready to hang it up and call it a day. But if Jesus approaches you with any kind of invitation, do yourself a favor and go with it. Venture out into the deep with Him. He never leaves us empty.

Think About It: Peter's experience of Jesus happened in the deep, not the shallow. To get the catch, you must go from the invitation to the application.

22

ONE MORE TIME

[Jesus asked,] "Who do you say that I am?" Simon Peter replied, "You are the Christ, the Son of the living God." And Jesus answered him, "Blessed are you, Simon Bar-Jonah! For flesh and blood has not revealed this to you, but my Father who is in heaven."

MATTHEW 16:15-17 ESV

I once had an entire week like Peter's horrible, no-good night of fishing (see the previous reading), and it fell, of all times, during a training camp with NFL Europe. After yet another bad practice, I was so fed up that I told both my dad and my coach, "I'm done. I'm taking the next flight home."

If not for the team requiring all departing players to have a physical exam, I would've been out of there that evening. Instead, I had to wait until the next day. True to form, my dad used that circumstance to challenge me: "Go back to practice one more time, son, and ask where God wants you."

I wasn't too interested in God's answer. Really, I just wanted to get out of Tampa, where training camp was held, and get home to Dallas. But I did attend the next practice. It wasn't good either. I cried through most of it, unable to hold back my emotions.

Finally, during a short breather between plays, I gave up and told God, "If You want me to stay, You'll have to give me a peace that surpasses understanding." And wouldn't you know it, the second my hand touched the turf for the next snap, I felt completely different. I'm not exaggerating. And right after I made the play, I turned to my coach and said, "I'm staying."

Over the next several months of the season in Europe, my place on the team was established. I became known as "Rev," for "Reverend," and seven of those guys I played ball with accepted Christ.

In a real sense, Peter and I had similar outcomes when we ventured back out into the waters with Jesus in the boat. Except that Peter didn't need a doctor's exam, a dad's challenge, *and* an overflow of peace for him to follow through on Christ's invitation.

You and I might not always relate to the men or women in the Bible who were an instant "Yes!" whenever God came calling. But I think we can all see ourselves in Peter's tiredness and discouragement. Still, he picked up his nets and tried again, simply because Jesus said so. If it was reason enough for the disciple upon whom Christ built His church (Matthew 16:18), it's reason enough for me.

Think About It: The place I wanted to give up was the place I needed to grow up. The same is true for you.

23

MARATHON MESSENGER

How delightful on the mountains are the feet of one who brings good news, who announces peace and brings good news of happiness, who announces salvation, and says to Zion, "Your God reigns!"

ISAIAH 52:7

In 1 Peter 2:9, the apostle says this of all believers: "You are a chosen people, a royal priesthood, a holy nation, a people for God's own possession." What's the purpose of our position and our placement as Christians? "So that you may proclaim the excellencies of Him who has called you out of darkness into His marvelous light."

That proclaiming thing is a big deal! Especially when it's great news. Just ask the original marathon man, Pheidippides.

He was a Greek military messenger known as a "day-long runner," and his purpose was to travel as far as necessary (sometimes more than a hundred miles) to communicate the message he'd been given. Legend has it that after the sorely outnumbered Greeks emerged victorious over Persia in the Battle of Marathon in 490 BC, our man "Phe" covered about 26 miles on foot from the battlefield to announce the victory to his countrymen in Athens.

Every follower of Jesus gets to likewise be a good-news messenger all day long and all life long through a *life of faith* and the *testimony of faith*. You don't have to live perfectly or communicate eloquently. But do give your all and be genuine. Paul freely admitted to the Christians in Corinth, "When I came to you, brothers and sisters, I did not come as someone superior in speaking ability or wisdom, as I proclaimed to you the testimony of God." He simply determined to speak "Jesus Christ, and Him crucified…in demonstration of the Spirit and of power" (1 Corinthians 2:1-2, 4).

You are not only a warrior in God's army but a witness. You're not just military but a messenger. A bearer of the best news. Run well, marathoners, so that both your mouth and your life may proclaim the victory of the One who called you into His service.

Think About It: Serving God means serving others. Bring the good news with you. Many are waiting on your arrival.

24

COURAGE OR COMPROMISE?

Be on guard. Stand firm in the faith.
Be courageous. Be strong.

1 CORINTHIANS 16:13 NLT

Quick quiz: Name somebody in the Bible who caved in to peer pressure or people-pleasing.

There was Aaron, fashioning a golden calf idol at the demands of the impatient and unruly Israelites (Exodus 32). Saul, admitting to the prophet Samuel, "I have violated the command of the Lord...because I feared the people and listened to their voice" (1 Samuel 15:24). King Herod killing John the Baptist because the woman he was infatuated with asked for it (Matthew 14:1-11), and later, inciting violence against Christians and arresting Peter because "it pleased the Jews" (Acts 12:3).

It's easy to call these people cowards until we turn the mirror on ourselves. Maybe you're not caving yet, but are you *inching* from your godly convictions to fit in or win approval? Talking behind your boss's back at work, maybe, or criticizing your spouse to your equally critical friends? Compromising your morals to keep your boyfriend or girlfriend happy?

You can do the cowardly thing, or you can draw on the Lord for strength and conviction. Hebrews 11 cites people like Moses's parents, who stood against the king's edict and took the necessary risks to protect their son (verse 23); Moses himself, who as an adult chose "rather to be mistreated with the people of God than to enjoy the fleeting pleasures of sin" (verse 25 ESV); and Rahab, who went against her own people to protect Israel's spies (verse 31). These faithful ones and so many others stood with God, believed God, and obeyed God in all kinds of circumstances (verses 32-38). You can too.

Inside this famous Bible chapter is a short but telling description. Verse 34 speaks of the ones who "were made strong out of weakness" (ESV). That's really what conviction is: letting the Spirit of God make you strong in situations where you might normally shrink back or where others are being weak.

Conviction, not compromise. Steadfast to the end. This is part of your heritage in the Lord. Hold the line and live to make Christ proud.

Think About It: Are you living for man's applause while heaven is quiet, or living for heaven's applause while man is quiet? Many times you can have both, but not always. Be careful what you choose.

25

THE POWER OF ONE

Oh, Lord God! You Yourself made the heavens and earth by Your great power and with Your outstretched arm. Nothing is too difficult for You.

JEREMIAH 32:17 HCSB

Assyria's king, Sennacherib, had already captured some of the fortified cities in Judah, but his main target lay ahead: Judah's capital, Jerusalem. Over many, many months, the king of Judah, Hezekiah, readied both the city and his people for war. He also strengthened their confidence with these words: "Do not fear or be dismayed because of the king of Assyria nor because of all the horde that is with him; for the One with us is greater than the one with him. With him is only an arm of flesh, but with us is the Lord our God to help us and to fight our battles" (2 Chronicles 32:7-8).

The phrase Hezekiah used, "arm of flesh," refers to manpower—the horde of men in Sennacherib's army. That's where the enemy's confidence resided. "On what are you basing your confidence?" mocked the Assyrian king. "Just as the gods of the peoples of the other lands did not rescue their people from my hand, so the god of Hezekiah will not rescue his people from my hand" (verses 10, 17 NIV).

By contrast, while Hezekiah didn't ignore the practical realities of defending the city against a future siege, he was more concerned with the superhuman power of One, the God of heaven. That's who he appealed to, the Commander of the angelic hosts. Judah's king prayed for the Almighty's help, and before Sennacherib could carry out his plans, God handled it. He sent just one angel from the army of heaven, who cut down "every warrior, commander, and officer in the camp of the king of Assyria" (verse 21).

With all his manpower gone, guess who suddenly lost his confidence? Scripture details that Sennacherib returned to his homeland, ashamed and disgraced.

The enemy likes to spout off, but God will not be mocked, and we shouldn't be moved—not by the enemy's plots, the personnel involved, or the onslaught of words. The outcome of our battle rests where our confidence rests: in the reality that our God is greater, and nothing is too difficult for Him!

Think About It: Look up Psalm 44:4-8 in your favorite Bible translation and make that your prayer today.

FIRST THINGS FIRST

One thing I do: forgetting what lies behind and reaching forward to what lies ahead, I press on toward the goal for the prize of the upward call of God in Christ Jesus.

PHILIPPIANS 3:13-14

If you ever played sports, your coach probably said in the pregame huddle, "Leave it all out there on the field!" Really, though, by then it's too late. Games are won in the weight room, and in the training room, and in practice by the players who have given their all *already*—before they ever step on the field of battle.

That's a biblical concept even more than an athletic one: We have to get uncomfortable if we want the prize.

Think of Abraham. What did God tell him to do before He delivered on His covenant promise? "Leave everything you know behind—your relatives, your country, and your father's house—and go where I tell you" (see Genesis 12:1-3). The victory comes after the sacrifice, not before.

I've heard many Christians get it backward. They say, "I'm just waiting on God to show up and show out, then I'll do what He's asked me to do." But you know what? God is waiting on *you* to show up and show out! At the point that you move, He'll move. He'll bring the firepower, making sure you get the win.

The Lord essentially told Abraham, "Before we get to the promise, before you taste the sweetness of victory, and before I start tossing the confetti, first things first: Will you give up your comfort to carry out what I've called you to do?"

God will get you to the good stuff if you'll give up all the other stuff. He's got the championship trophy waiting, with your name engraved on it. Heaven's cloud of witnesses is already assembled, ready to congratulate you. But you must decide whether—and when—you'll leave your will, your way, your perspective, your history, your comfort, and your preferences behind for the sake of the call.

Abraham did it before he ever set foot in the promised land, just like so many other Christians over the centuries. It's your turn now.

Think About It: To experience the confetti of greatness that God holds in His hands, you have to quit thinking *comfort* and start thinking *calling*.

27

MAKE AN IMPRESSION

You are a letter of Christ… written not with ink but with the Spirit of the living God, not on tablets of stone but on tablets of human hearts.

2 CORINTHIANS 3:3

Every generation has some kind of cultural war to fight, though probably no generation in history has been so self-absorbed as ours. There are enough social media platforms alone (the tip of the digital iceberg) to tempt even the most devout Christian to serve the human trinity—*me, myself, and I*—rather than the spiritual one.

So how do you know you're serving God and not yourself? Simple. Somebody is impacted. That's how my sister Chrystal Evans Hurst defines it. If you've been touched by the life of another Christian, she says, then that person's influence has reached your heart. Even more, if you've been touched by the life of another Christian, then in their life and yours is the ripple effect of *Christ's* influence.

That's the type of influencer we should want to be—one who, whether in word or deed, does "everything in the name of the Lord Jesus" (Colossians 3:17).

The apostle Paul would have agreed. Not wanting the believers in Rome (a culturally driven city if ever there was one) to be conformed to this world, but to reflect Christ, he wrote, "I urge you, brothers and sisters, by the mercies of God, to present your bodies as a living and holy sacrifice, acceptable to God" (Romans 12:1). Paul pointed directly to our divine example in a different letter: "Have this attitude in yourselves which was also in Christ Jesus, who...emptied Himself by taking the form of a bond-servant" (Philippians 2:5-7). The apostle specifically stated, "Do nothing from selfishness or empty conceit, but with humility consider one another as more important than yourselves; do not merely look out for your own personal interests, but also for the interests of others" (verses 3-4).

The easy thing in a culture like ours is to just go along and glorify ourselves in hopes of obtaining followers and influence. But Jesus led by example, and so must we. Strive to leave an imprint in your generation through your service, not your selfishness. The true influencers live by this simple principle.

Think About It: The apostle Paul had social media too! "Follow me as I follow Christ" (1 Corinthians 11:1 MEV). He knew what to do with his followers. Do you?

28

COUNT ON GOD

I am praying to you because I know you will answer.

PSALM 17:6 NLT

When you pray, are you inclined toward doubt and distrust? Or do you have the mindset of the psalmist in today's verse: "I am praying to you because I know you will answer"? In Psalm 130:5 in the New Living Translation, the poet says, "I am counting on the LORD; yes, I am counting on him."

Serving the Lord and being obedient to Him are ways we actively practice trust, but I say, let's go a step further and approach God expectantly, as the One in our lives who loves saying yes. That's what King Saul's son Jonathan did. In 1 Samuel 14:6 we read that, one day, Jonathan urged his armor bearer to come with him to the Philistine outpost, adding, "Perhaps the LORD will act in our behalf. Nothing can hinder the LORD from saving, whether by many or by few" (NIV). And evidently his armor bearer was of the same mind because he replied, "Do all that you have in mind…Go ahead; I am with you heart and soul" (verse 7 NIV).

Here's the key. Jonathan's attitude was "Why not? Perhaps

the Lord will act in our favor." His attitude was "Let's go explore, in case God has something for us to do." He didn't assume the negative. He viewed God as being more likely to say yes than no.

Now think of how you pray about the horizons ahead of you. As you're looking out over the landscape of your life and the Holy Spirit is bringing possibilities to mind, are you coming to God with a positive expectation or a negative inclination? All too often we shut Him down just as He's getting started, and then we wonder why we're not seeing any traction in our faith.

Have you been praying, and He's nudging you to explore something new, or clearly directing you to *go for it*? You can move forward, assuming, "Perhaps You will act in my favor, God," or you can stay put, telling yourself, "Probably He won't." But my Bible (and yours!) says that when God is for us, nothing can stop us (Romans 8:31). Nothing, that is, except for our own doubt. Pray with expectancy and count on God to give you His best.

Think About It: A flourishing faith doesn't shut down God. A flourishing faith opens up to all His possibilities and lets Him be God.

29

MY PORTION

"The Lord is my portion," says my soul, "therefore I wait for Him." The Lord is good to those who await Him, to the person who seeks Him.

LAMENTATIONS 3:24-25

The book of Lamentations is a collection of sorrow-filled, poetic reflections on the destruction of ancient Jerusalem by the Babylonians. More broadly, it expresses some of the hard realities of life, especially the things we ask and feel and say to ourselves—and to God—when it seems our lives are in ruin. As a matter of fact, Lamentations 3:17-18 is a cry of the heart that any of us can relate to: "My soul has been excluded from peace; I have forgotten happiness. So I say, 'My strength has failed, and so has my hope from the Lord.'"

Which makes it all the more ironic that, near the center of this short book, almost like the bull's-eye on a target, we find a defining statement of faith from its writer, the "weeping prophet," Jeremiah. In the middle of five chapters recounting Jeremiah's enormous grief and remorse for Jerusalem and the sins of its people, God gives His servant the strength to rise above the circumstances and simultaneously *proclaim* the Lord's goodness and *claim* the Lord as his forever portion and sufficiency. The Geneva Study Bible commentary on Lamentations 3:24 explains the verse this way: "The godly put their whole confidence in God, and therefore look for no other inheritance" or provision.

If you're still waiting for resolution...breakthrough...restoration...victory in your adversity, then you're waiting because God is still working. He's back there in the kitchen, busily preparing to reveal an even bigger portion of Himself and His handiwork to you. David experienced this firsthand, celebrating: "You prepare a table before me in the presence of my enemies; You have anointed my head with oil; my cup overflows. Certainly goodness and faithfulness will follow me all the days of my life" (Psalm 23:5-6).

Romans 8:28 promises that we can "know[!] that in all things God works for the good of those who love him, who have been called according to his purpose" (NIV). So take heart, my friends, and keep seeking Him. Because as I like to say: *If it's not good yet, God's not done yet.*

Think About It: Waiting is always hard, but with God, we must continue to trust that it will be well worth the wait.

30

OAK TREES AND IRONSIDES

They will be called oaks of righteousness, the planting of the LORD, that He may be glorified.

ISAIAH 61:3

Oak trees often live for hundreds of years. While most of them shed their leaves each fall and regrow them in the spring, one variety is nearly evergreen: the Southern live oak. During a few weeks each year, it sheds and grows new leaves so that it's almost never without foliage. Southern live oaks are also able to survive in less-than-ideal environments where other trees struggle to grow, and their wood is super strong.

To understand just how strong, you've heard of the Navy vessel nicknamed "Old Ironsides," right? Well, it got that name in the War of 1812—not because it was made of iron, but because it stayed afloat despite numerous cannon shots. (Experts say those cannonballs were 18 pounds!)

Do you know why the ship survived the onslaught? Because its hull was built from Southern live oak. Its hull withstood enemy attack *like iron.*

What a great picture of our potential strength through Christ! Not only does the Lord make us capable of an enduring, all-season faith, but in Him we also can keep producing leaves and strong shade into old age and beyond. I've seen this firsthand across my family tree—from my grandparents through my parents, aunts and uncles, and in so many of the older saints in the church.

The one who delights in God's Word and who meditates on it day and night, wrote the psalmist, is both a blessing and will be blessed. "He is like a tree planted by streams of water that yields its fruit in its season, and its leaf does not wither" (Psalm 1:3 ESV).

Christians are made for this. Made to produce good shade and good fruit in abundance, over and over again. Through Christ we become oaks of righteousness—a strong shade and source of life for others for as long as we live.

Think About It: Being rooted in Christ makes us ever-growing and evergreen.

31

AT FACE VALUE

Praise the Lord, my soul, and forget not all his benefits— who forgives all your sins...who redeems your life from the pit and crowns you with love and compassion.

PSALM 103:2-4 NIV

Among the many benefits of following the Lord cited in Psalm 103 are these: He "forgives all your sins" and "crowns you with love and compassion" (NIV). First John 1:9 echoes this, saying, "If we confess our sins, He is faithful and just to forgive us our sins and to cleanse us from all unrighteousness" (NKJV). So does Romans 8:1-2: "No condemnation now exists for those in Christ Jesus, because the Spirit's law of life in Christ Jesus has set you free from the law of sin and of death" (HCSB).

I've highlighted only a few love-and-forgiveness verses here, but as you read through the Bible, you'll see how representative these are. Every time sin is spoken of, God's remedy in Christ is presented as a complete solution. It's not for "these" sins or "those" people but not others. There's no fine print to read, and you don't have to buy an upgrade either. Everything was paid for up front. You can take the words of the Lord at face value: He forgives *all* your sins and cleanses you from *all* unrighteousness. Once your righteousness is in Christ, *no* condemnation is attached to you any longer. You are set *free*, with nothing being held over your head and nothing tethering you to your past mistakes.

When God says it, you can believe it. And you can celebrate it. Just look at the picture in Psalm 103:4 of the Lord crowning us with love and compassion. The coronation of King Charles in 2023 showed us what an event a crowning is in a kingdom. It's a whole lot of pomp and circumstance and ceremony, a huge cause for celebration.

Spiritually, you and I can take joy in knowing that God doesn't begrudgingly bestow these gifts. Probably every one of us has experienced the feeling of being presented with a bare-minimum gift because somebody felt obligated to give it. Not the Lord. He delights in crowning the repentant with His love and compassion. And we get to glory in His pure and total forgiveness.

In all of this, we are a people most blessed.

Think About It: The greatest gift a sinner can receive is God's love and compassion. Don't leave those gifts unwrapped. Believe in Christ so that God's gifts can be your experience.

32

SHOW ME

The hearing ear and the seeing eye,
the Lord *has made them both.*

PROVERBS 20:12 NKJV

For many Christians, accepting the forgiveness of God at face value is easier said than done. One reason is because the majority of us humans (in fact, two out of every three people) are more the "show me" type—visual learners who need a picture or an image for the truth to sink in.

Fair enough. If you have trouble believing what God says about your status with Him, then here are some visuals to back up His words.

Anytime guilt or shame from the past is trying to get the best of you, picture *a white cross* like the ones all over Arlington National Cemetery in Washington, DC. Jesus surrendered Himself, shedding His blood and giving His life to ensure that you could live free, with your sins completely washed clean.

Or picture *a beating heart.* He did this for no reason other than His sheer love for you and His desire to spend eternity with you. There is no greater love than this (John 15:13).

Or, for those of you who played team sports, picture *a*

substitute entering the game and finishing it out for you because your injury—in this case, your sin—made it impossible for you to do it yourself. That's the meaning of Hebrews 9:12: "By his own blood he entered in once into the holy place, having obtained eternal redemption for us" (KJV).

Or picture *a receipt* showing "Paid in full." First John 2:1-2 spells it out: "If anyone sins, we have an Advocate with the Father, Jesus Christ the righteous; and He Himself is the propitiation for our sins." He covered your entire debt. When Jesus died, His payment for your sins was credited to your account. And when He rose again, the payment went through.

Or picture *a clean bill of health* from your doctor. Christ has made you whole. By Him, the prophetic promise of Isaiah 53:4-5 has been thoroughly fulfilled: "It was our sicknesses that He Himself bore, and our pains that He carried...The punishment for our well-being was laid upon Him, and by His wounds we are healed."

However you need to visualize God's forgiveness, see it and believe!

Think About It: John the Baptist gave us one of the Bible's purest pictures of Christ when he exclaimed, "Behold, the Lamb of God who takes away the sin of the world!" (John 1:29). What imagery will help you behold Him and His forgiveness for you?

33

NEVER ALONE

A wise man is strong, and a person of knowledge increases power. For by wise guidance you will wage war, and in an abundance of counselors there is victory.

PROVERBS 24:5-6

The historic military figure Sun Tzu is best known for his book *The Art of War*, in which he wrote, "He will win whose army is animated by the same spirit throughout all its ranks." General Tzu also wrote, "The art of war teaches us to rely not on the likelihood of the enemy's not coming, but on our own readiness to receive him; not on the chance of his not attacking, but rather on the fact that we have made our position unassailable."

Do you want to know one of the best ways to position yourself for victory in any battle according to God's Book? Don't fight alone. Surround yourself with fellow warriors who believe greatly in the power of the gospel, who loyally follow the Lord's commands, and who never enter battle without their spiritual armor and sword.

Besides the fellowship and teaching on the weekends within your local church, I encourage you to get as much training as you can by attending Bible studies or classes and participating in a small group. I also recommend seeking out the camaraderie of spiritual friends such as mentors, prayer partners, and accountability partners. Having this army around you won't safeguard you from every form of trouble—because in this world, Jesus said we *will* have trouble (John 16:33). But if, by the wisdom and counsel of many Spirit-led comrades, you can avoid inviting trouble and learn to stand firm in the Lord, that too is victory.

Paul advised one of his mentees, Timothy, to not only "flee from youthful lusts" but to "pursue righteousness, faith, love, and peace *with those who call on the Lord from a pure heart*" (2 Timothy 2:22). Locking arms and aligning yourself with prayerful, God-honoring, like-minded believers is positioning yourself to experience the strength that exists in numbers. Even more, it is positioning yourself to go to war—and win.

Think About It: The enemy loves to see you in isolation because he knows one single cadet won't stand a chance against his infantry. Joining forces is both wisdom and protection.

34

GET YOUR STEPS IN

Whoever says he abides in [Jesus] ought to walk in the same way in which he walked.

1 JOHN 2:6 ESV

Remember when the activity trackers for your wrist first came out, before smartwatches hit it big? Seemed like everybody was wearing a Fitbit or something like it and obsessing over getting in their steps for the day. Doctors have always recommended walking as a great low-impact exercise—improving heart health, aiding in weight loss, and increasing physical stamina.

Our Great Physician makes an even stronger claim. He says walking is actually the perfect *high-impact* exercise for every believer. It increases your heart for God, helps you lose the weight of sin and worry, and increases your spiritual stamina. And, bonus, it also enhances your relational health, bringing you closer to God and others. So make it a point to get these steps in every day:

- Walk according to the Spirit, not the flesh (Romans 8:4; Galatians 5:16).
- Walk by faith, not by sight (2 Corinthians 5:7).

- Walk in the good works God has prepared for you (Ephesians 2:10).
- Walk in love, just as Christ loved you (Ephesians 5:2).
- Walk as the wise do, making the most of your time, because the days are evil (Ephesians 5:15-16).
- Walk in a manner worthy of the Lord, bearing fruit in every good work and increasing in the knowledge of God (Colossians 1:10).
- Walk in Christ, rooted and built up in Him and established in the faith, abounding in thanksgiving (Colossians 2:6-7).
- Walk in the truth (3 John 3:3-4).

C'mon now, no putting it off! It's time to get our steps in. Let's get going!

Think About It: You can dream, hope, visualize, imagine, and have confidence in where God is taking you, but unless you take the steps, you'll never get there.

FIRST RESPONSE

"I am the Lord's servant," Mary answered.
"May your word to me be fulfilled."

LUKE 1:38 NIV

Something that matters for every Christian is how responsive we are to God's instruction and direction in our lives.

I've been known to be, shall we say, headstrong at times. While I was playing in the NFL, God started nudging me toward full-time ministry. But I resisted. As much as I loved and respected my dad, Pastor Tony Evans, no way did I want to be a preacher! I was determined to keep grinding despite being cut from teams, traded multiple times, and carried off the field with injuries.

The Lord even tried getting through to me through my discerning wife, who, after a series of these setbacks, suggested that maybe it was time for me to hang up the cleats and apply to seminary. Nope! Nothing was going to deter me from my plan. Then one day, I tore my Achilles tendon during a workout, and that is how my playing days ended.

Like Jacob, I wrestled with God, and He changed how I walked (Genesis 32:24-32). Hopefully you're less headstrong than me. Nevertheless, every one of us needs to evaluate how much it takes to get our attention. Does God have to go to Jonah-like lengths before you'll listen? Are you an exhaust-all-my-options-first kind of person? Or are you more of an Isaiah: "Here I am. Send me" (Isaiah 6:8 NLT)?

After this experience of mine, I have even more respect for Mary, the mother of Jesus. Her first response to the angel's news that she would conceive and give birth to God's Son wasn't "Nope! Pick somebody else," or "How will this affect my dream of marrying Joseph?" She essentially replied, "Though I don't understand how this will all go down, I'll serve You, Lord, in whatever way You want" (see Luke 1:38).

May you and I be that responsive to God's desires for us today.

Think About It: Be careful not to reject your own legacy by living with spiritual hesitancy to God's voice.

36

BEYOND THE CALL

To Him who is able to do far more abundantly beyond all that we ask or think, according to the power that works within us, to Him be the glory in the church and in Christ Jesus.

EPHESIANS 3:20-21

It's human nature to blame God whenever we're on the losing end of one of life's battles. After all, He's God. Our wonder-working, all-powerful God. He can do anything He decides. Intervene anytime He wants. Vanquish any enemy. Silence any opposition. In short, He *could have* altered the outcome in our favor, exactly as we prayed...but He didn't. What then?

In those times when I'm prone to blaming God, I'm learning to redirect my thoughts, even though my emotions are running strong.

The first thing I do is examine myself: Did I go to the Lord for wisdom at each step, or was I selfishly pursuing my agenda, hoping He'd just sign off on it? Have I been prideful or unrepentant or slow to move on something in my life that He's been quietly urging me to deal with (like my call to ministry)?

Second, I remind myself of His infinite ability to creatively accomplish His purpose in our lives once we finally surrender to Him. After I tore my Achilles tendon as an NFL player, I thought that was it. *Game over. Career over.* But just two years later, I found myself standing in the tunnel with the Dallas Cowboys, waiting for my first regular-season game. Not as a player but as the team's chaplain. As I described it in my book *Fighting Your Battles*, "God turned my misery within the game of football into my ministry within the game of football."[4] What's more, I now get to point people to God year-round through the church and books and speaking opportunities—sharing the gospel far beyond what I could have done as one player in a locker room.

Could God have prevented my injury and directed my steps in some other way? Sure. Just like He could've prevented what has happened to you. But the fact that He didn't just may be a call from Him. A call to press in and open yourself to what else He has in mind for you.

Think About It: With God, your greatest misery can become your greatest ministry. Trust Him to work it out.

37

SMALL WINS

Thanks be to God, who gives us the victory through our Lord Jesus Christ.

1 CORINTHIANS 15:57

As I've shared, after five years in the NFL, I suffered an injury during a workout that ended my playing career.

After my surgery came the work of physical rehab, where, instead of going for touchdowns, I was just hoping to gain a little more strength and extension in my leg. My wife, Kanika, who is a trained physical therapist, would tell you: When you're recovering from an injury, small wins can be good wins too.

I know how much I like the big wins. Really, who doesn't? Those are the ones we love to talk about for the rest of our lives. But the practice of rejoicing in little victories is maybe just as important to the building up of our faith as those occasions when God shows up in a major way and shows off.

In your battle today, look for the small wins—

- A perfectly hot cup of coffee or tea.
- What somebody does for you at work that eases your load.

- A "thinking of you" text from someone you weren't expecting to hear from.
- Baby steps of progress in an area you've been focused on.
- The comment your kid makes that shows you, *He's getting it. She's paying attention after all.*
- A word from Scripture that reaches straight to your heart.
- A surprise compliment.
- The beautiful sunset God sets in the sky.
- A short checkout line or drive-through lane that saves you time.

God gives these glimmers of hope every day to encourage you in your journey. Every one of them points to our greatest hope and strength in life: the victory we have through our salvation in Christ.

Think About It: Especially in the heart of one who is thankful, many little wins can amount to a major victory. Just give it time.

TRIAL RUN

Do you not know? Have you not heard? The Everlasting God, the LORD, the Creator of the ends of the earth does not become weary or tired...He gives strength to the weary, and to the one who lacks might He increases power... Those who wait for the LORD will gain new strength.

ISAIAH 40:28-29, 31

Until I had surgery for my Achilles injury, I couldn't put any weight on that leg at all. Post-surgery, I started rehabbing right away. It took a while, but after putting in all the work to strengthen the tendon a little at a time, I was ready to try walking without crutches. The question was: Would it be able to bear my weight?

I took one step, two steps, another, and another—all good. Months later, I put it to the full test: I ran. And by then, my leg was strong enough to bear my weight at full speed.

The pain of suffering will force you to ask a similar question of your faith: "Can I really put all the weight of my life on God?" You want to know if He can safely absorb your emotions, bear you up in your circumstances, and empower you to run with joy...without failing.

To get to that critical answer for yourself, it's probably going to take some time. You'll need to work up to it. Understanding the need for progression, the Lord doesn't use all-or-nothing verbs in Isaiah 40. He speaks of *increasing* and *renewing* the strength of the weak until they can run without tiring, until they can walk without fainting. In effect, the lesser pains and struggles of life are chances to exercise patience, build up your character, and strengthen your trust in God *before* the full-weight trial run.

You'll likely have hundreds of opportunities to test your faith in smaller ways, but the day *will* come when you'll have to really put yourself out there and see if it holds. On that day, you'll either walk in faith or you'll faint. You'll either run, or you'll be too tired to try.

There's no need to dread that day. You can be ready for it, like I was. And just as I had people around to support me in case I faltered, God will be right beside you, ready to give you His shoulder should you need to steady yourself.

Your smaller times of testing aren't meant as nuisances. They're not God's attempts to frustrate you. He's preparing you to run, to soar above difficulties, and to walk and not faint (Isaiah 40:31).

Think About It: Like the old hymn says, every time you work your faith and try out your trust in the Lord, you're building up "strength for today and bright hope for tomorrow." Great is God's faithfulness.

39

GIFTED!

From [Christ] the whole body, joined and held together by every supporting ligament, grows and builds itself up in love, as each part does its work.

EPHESIANS 4:16 NIV

Maybe you were never one of those gifted kids in school, but I have some great news: In the church, *every* believer is *gifted*.

That's one of the things the Holy Spirit makes sure of as soon as a person is saved. "There are varieties of gifts, but the same Spirit. And there are varieties of ministries, and the same Lord...But to each one is given the manifestation of the Spirit for the common good" (1 Corinthians 12:4-5, 7).

Those spiritual gifts are an important way that you beautify the bride of Christ and build up the body of Christ—the church. But like our beauty routines and exercise regimens, we always have the choice of "Will I or won't I?" Whether or not you grace and grow others with your gifts is a question you have to answer.

Now I'll admit, sometimes it's the people *inside* the church who get in the way. They turn ministry into a competition, seeing who can one-up the next person. You know these cats. They have their little worship-team clique, or they're insecure about anyone new joining their ministry because you might dare to come along and shake things up with your fresh ideas. But if nobody is preventing you, then what's stopping you? As a pastor, I get to see how beautifully it all works together and how important each person is.

Those who make meals for the sick or the grieving, or prepare the coffee for adult Sunday school...you're a *gift*!

The ones who care for babies during the service, giving weary parents a chance to participate...you are a *gift* to those moms and dads.

Anyone who helps people get parked, shows newcomers where the bathrooms are, prints out the bulletins, or sets up the microphones...you're a *gift* to your church.

Those who tidy up a classroom or collect the trash after the service or contribute to the mission fund...what a *gift* you are to the body and the bride of Christ!

This Sunday, put your giftedness to work. Start using what you've got for Christ's glory. Through you, others will see and know and find strength in the One you are serving together.

Think About It: Need some further encouragement that you are important for your fellow believers? Read 1 Corinthians 12 and spend some time meditating on its message, considering what you can do to enhance and strengthen the people around you in *their* service to Christ.

40

ZERO PERCENT

He who sent Me is true; and the things which I heard from Him, these I say to the world...I say these things as the Father instructed Me. And He who sent Me is with Me; He has not left Me alone, for I always do the things that are pleasing to Him.

JOHN 8:26, 28-29

If you're familiar with those body-language experts on YouTube, they're all about dissecting the speech, physical movements, and facial expressions of people who are being interviewed, to analyze the person's level of truthfulness. And two of the things they pay special attention to are a person's blink patterns, and if and when they start to stutter. (Those of us who have raised, coached, or taught children or teenagers use some of the same indicators intuitively, am I right?) Typically, the person who can look you straight in the eye and answer questions without stuttering is telling the truth.

That's something I love about Jesus's words as He was being questioned by haters and followers alike in John 8. His statements throughout this chapter are a powerful picture of truthfulness. Jesus didn't just explain but declare—without stuttering or blinking!—that He and His Father in heaven are one…and 100 percent legit. In verse 12, He even announced, "I am the Light of the world; the one who follows Me will not walk in the darkness." Then He basically went on to say, "And you can take that to the bank. Just ask Dad."

Truer words have never been spoken! And when we're battling the deception, darkness, or disease of this world, we need truth more than ever.

For that battle you're in right now, start fortifying yourself with Jesus's words throughout the Gospel of John, and *believe Him*! Not only is the One you serve 100 percent true in who He is and what He says, but as Jesus verified in verses 31-32, "If you continue in My word, then you are truly My disciples; and you will know the truth, and the truth will set you free."

Think About It: Jesus is not only with you always, but He will never, ever lie to you.

41

SILENCING THE ROAR

Be on the alert. Your adversary,
the devil, prowls around like a roaring lion,
seeking someone to devour.

1 PETER 5:8

I can guarantee that you and I have heard the enemy's roar.

In some situations, it's loud and persistent, like Goliath's, who exited his tent twice a day to shout the same threats day after day. In other situations, the enemy's voice is quieter but still unrelenting: The voice of shame. Scarcity. False blame. Rejection. Feelings of uselessness or futility. It may come at you as you recall the words of someone you grew up with, are married to, or once dated. Or possibly in the actions of someone from the past who was supposed to be looking out for you and instead took advantage of you.

Sometimes the enemy's voice is in the cravings of temptation or addiction. Or the striving for Pinterest-level perfectionism. But the worst of all is when the enemy gets inside our heads. Whether those voices are shouting or whispering, the lies can become so entrenched that we start repeating *to ourselves* the things we've been told. And soon enough, like the army of

Israel until David came along, we just stand by, listening and backing down a little more each day (1 Samuel 17).

Satan loves it when we get in that headspace. It makes his job that much easier.

Let's not do the work for him. Let's not defeat ourselves by putting the lies on repeat like a familiar song. Our enemy likes to prowl around and roar like a lion, but we serve the Lord of the battle, the Lion of Judah. He has defeated sin and death and will one day return to earth, silencing Satan once and for all. Until then, you don't have to sit there and take it. By the authority of Jesus, you can stand firm and rebuke the devil to his face. He's going to back down once you start fighting back in the name of Jesus. And when he sees you pull out the sword of God's Word, don't be surprised if he turns and runs. Satan knows the source of your power—and he doesn't stand a chance.

Think About It: Without God's Word, you only have the enemy's voice, and that's dangerous. Meditate on His Word so you can fight.

42

THE HIGH LIFE

See how great a love the Father has given us,
that we would be called children of God; and in fact we are.

1 JOHN 3:1

Have you heard of Anna Sorokin? The Russian-born emigrant from Germany moved to New York as an adult, changed her last name, and began bragging to her business connections that she was a rich heiress, when in fact, she was the daughter of working-class parents. Sorokin was so intent on experiencing the high life that she falsified documents and financial records, defrauding and deceiving many of her associates—from lending institutions and the plush hotels where she stayed, to friends and acquaintances. Her thievery landed her in prison and publicly exposed her for the pretender she was.

For Christians, we have no need to pretend. First John 3:1 is definitive: We aren't just called children of the Most High God; we are, *in fact,* His children. Thus we have unrestricted access to the high life in Him, both now and in eternity.

God the Father went to every length to ensure that those who receive His Son as Lord and Savior are instantly accepted as family and made permanent heirs of His kingdom. Ephesians 1 is all the documentation you need. (We will review this chapter more closely in the next reading.) It lays out "the hope to which he has called you, the riches of his glorious inheritance in his holy people, and his incomparably great power for us who believe" (verses 18-19 NIV).

These profound gifts were made yours when God the Father "raised Christ from the dead and seated him at his right hand in the heavenly realms, far above all rule and authority, power and dominion, and every name that is invoked, not only in the present age but also in the one to come" (verses 20-21 NIV).

What does this mean for you? No matter the status of your earthly family, you have a faith family extending through Christ's worldwide church, all the way to the throne of heaven. You're also an heir of the highest kingdom—and you have the family name to show for it, secured by the blood of Christ. That makes you royalty. Wear your name with confidence.

Think About It: Do you know who your Daddy is? Then act like it.

YOU'RE OFFICIAL!

The Spirit you received brought about your adoption to sonship. And by him we cry, "Abba, Father." The Spirit himself testifies with our spirit that we are God's children.

ROMANS 8:15-16 NIV

Ephesians 1 contains your adoption paperwork—officially and divinely signed, sealed, and delivered in the pages of Scripture by Father, Son, and Holy Spirit. You can rest easy with this sacred "documentation" in hand, knowing the Lord won't ever write you out of His will. Once you've been included as His son or daughter, you're in.

These resounding words, some of which I've italicized for further meditation, verify how completely you are loved, how thoroughly God planned for you, and how decisively He chose you as His own.

> Even before he made the world, *God loved us and chose us in Christ* to be holy and without fault in his eyes. God decided in advance to adopt us... through Jesus Christ. *This is what he wanted to do, and it gave him great pleasure.* So we praise

> God for the glorious grace he has poured out on us who belong to his dear Son. *He is so rich in kindness and grace that he purchased our freedom with the blood of his Son and forgave our sins.* He has showered his kindness on us, along with all wisdom and understanding…Furthermore, *because we are united with Christ, we have received an inheritance from God*…When you believed in Christ, he identified you as his own by giving you the Holy Spirit, whom he promised long ago. *The Spirit is God's guarantee that he will give us the inheritance he promised and that he has purchased us to be his own people* (Ephesians 1:4-8, 11, 13-14 NLT).

It doesn't get more real than that. You can claim your name as a Christian because you're family now, and heaven itself has announced the news. Believer, rejoice.

Think About It: Should the devil ever try to rob you of your identity, open your Bible and rebuke him with these words: *I am wanted. I am loved. And I belong.*

44

IN ALL YOUR WAYS

Trust in the Lord *with all your heart*
and do not lean on your own understanding.
In all your ways acknowledge Him,
and He will make your paths straight.

PROVERBS 3:5-6

Today's passage reminds us to seek the Lord in *all* our ways. We really need to take Him seriously in this. We miss out on so much if we treat God like He is separate from every other part of life.

In Proverbs 3, we're instructed to seek the Lord for our reputation, our direction, our production, and our protection—and that's just the short list! So to consult God about practical things like your budget, your schedule, your career decisions, your parenting dilemmas, your dating life, the tough conversations you need to have...isn't crazy. It's wisdom!

For me, a husband and the father of five active kids, I involve Him by going to Him about ways I can love my wife even more intentionally and striving to train our kids by the fruit of His Spirit rather than reacting to them in the flesh. I'm aware of wildly successful entrepreneurs who seek God's will long and hard in prayer—sometimes praying for weeks or months or more—before making major business or personal decisions. A friend of a friend, a pastor's wife, organizes her day around the Lord, beginning with her morning routines and disciplines, rather than trying to "fit Him in" somewhere.

The point is, we center our lives on God; He doesn't revolve around us. With Him as our sun, you and I can be drawing on His infinite wisdom all day, every day, in every way.

No matter what you're busy with, let your faith flow into your daily life, saturating it like water from a garden hose. Consult God and keep looping Him in until you get an answer accompanied by His unwavering peace. I'm telling you, once you start relating to the Lord as if He matters in all matters (not just in times of crisis or what you deem to be "spiritual concerns"), you'll hear Jesus more through His Word. You'll feel the Father's love more consistently. And you'll see the Holy Spirit at work more and more in your life, directing your every decision.

Think About It: If you lean a ladder on something, you want to make sure it's something that can hold you up. That's why you lean the ladder of your life on God and not on yourself.

45

PROXIMITY

Do not be wise in your own eyes; fear the Lord and turn away from evil. It will be healing to your body and refreshment to your bones.

PROVERBS 3:7-8

W*as he an overly confident kind of guy, or was he naive?* That's what I wonder about Abraham's nephew Lot when I read his story in Genesis 13–14 and 19.

After moving to the area of the Negev at the Lord's command, Abram let his younger relative choose which part he wanted to settle in. Lot apparently didn't think about it for long. He "looked around and saw that the whole plain of the Jordan toward Zoar was well watered, like the garden of the Lord, like the land of Egypt" (Genesis 13:10 NIV). And—*done!* Decision made. He took his flocks and his family eastward to live among the cities of the plain.

But here's the catch. Moving east meant he "pitched his tents near Sodom" (Genesis 13:12 NIV), a city well known as a dwelling place of "exceedingly wicked sinners against the Lord" (verse 13). By Genesis 14:12, Lot was "living in Sodom." By Genesis 19:1, Lot was "sitting at the gate of Sodom"—a meeting place for local leaders. He moved closer and closer to this evil place until he was living and doing business inside of it.

Though he and his family did not participate in the sins of Sodom, their *proximity* to its depravity proved disastrous, costing Lot his home, his wife, and a godly legacy. (Read all of Genesis 19 for the rest of the story.) His life just goes to show that unless you turn your back on evil completely, you'll be tempted to turn toward it. That's human nature—and the nature of darkness. It's just too easy to get drawn in and dragged down if we're anywhere in the vicinity of sin.

Stop toying with the tension. Stop teasing the lines between good and evil like you're the one who won't be caught in the web of consequences. You've been given the power of choice. Pick yourself up and relocate if you need to, putting as much distance between you and wickedness as possible.

"In Christ Jesus you who previously were far away have been brought near by the blood of Christ," wrote Paul (Ephesians 2:13). Plain and simple, *this* is the proximity we were purposed for.

Think About It: Proximity + Christ = Fulfillment and Purpose. Proximity + Culture = Failure and Pain. You know which equation works. Apply that one, and don't look back.

46

WITH DISTINCTION

Do not be mismatched with unbelievers; for what do righteousness and lawlessness share together, or what does light have in common with darkness?... "Therefore, come out from their midst and be separate," says the Lord... "And I will be a father to you, and you shall be sons and daughters to Me."

2 CORINTHIANS 6:14, 17-18

Lot's life is a lesson in how careful we should be in our association with the world, but so is Abraham's. While Lot situated himself within the wickedness of Sodom, made friends in Sodom, and did business in Sodom, his uncle Abram located in Hebron, not too far from what would one day become the city of Jerusalem, and devoted himself to the Lord.

That's one major difference between the two men. Here's another: Abram would not affiliate himself with the wicked even when the wicked wanted to affiliate with him. For example, after Abram and his small force of men caught up with and defeated regional marauders who had taken some of his family members captive, "the king of Sodom went out to meet him" upon his return (Genesis 14:17) and proposed sharing the spoils (verse 21). Abram refused, wanting no one but the one true God to be seen as his source of blessing: "I have sworn an oath to the LORD, God Most High, Creator of heaven and earth, that I will accept nothing belonging to you, not even a thread or the strap of a sandal, so that you will never be able to say, 'I made Abram rich'" (verses 22-23 NIV).

This is what it looks like to live "with distinction" in this world. The Lord warns, "Do not become partners with [the sons of disobedience]...Do not participate in the useless deeds of darkness, but instead even expose them; for it is disgraceful even to speak of the things which are done by them in secret" (Ephesians 5:7, 11-12). He also urges us to live carefully, "not as unwise people but as wise, making the most of [our] time, because the days are evil" (Ephesians 5:15-16).

We separate ourselves, not with an attitude of superiority, but with sincerity in our life with God. I'm telling you, if the people around us can't tell there's something positively different about us, then you and I had better check ourselves. After all, our calling is from above, and our "citizenship is in heaven" (Philippians 3:20). It's high time we start acting like it.

Think About It: You can't run at top speed for the purposes of God in a field full of fallen people. You will only find yourself tripping with every step.

WHY?

In [God's] great mercy he has given us new birth into a living hope through the resurrection of Jeus Christ from the dead, and into an inheritance that can never perish, spoil or fade. This inheritance is kept in heaven for you.

1 PETER 1:3-4 NIV

Between 2017 and 2019, eight of my relatives passed away. My wife and I also grieved four miscarriages before we ever held our first baby. Reading Judges 6:13 always takes me back to those couple of years when, one by one, the tolls of sadness accumulated, culminating in my mom's cancer diagnosis.

For months, our family, our church, and prayer warriors from seemingly everywhere fought fiercely on our knees, believing God would heal her. Instead, the cancer progressed, and on December 30, 2019, Lois Evans passed away.

In the days surrounding her death, I fought with my own grief and confusion at God's decision. I wrestled as a pastor too, sounding a lot like Gideon: "If the Lord is with us, why then has all this happened to us? And where are all His miracles which our fathers told us about…?'" (Judges 6:13).

I went at God with my frustration because I was angry: "This was the opportunity for You to show Your glory. You could've raised my mom up. Taken away the cancer. Where were You?"

Well, let me tell you, the Holy Spirit quickly brought to mind some of the truths I'd lost sight of.

For example, the fact that I don't get to tell God how to get His glory. I was approaching Him with a sense of entitlement, like He owed me something, when in reality, I owe Him everything for making a way for each of us to escape the pit of hell.

And the fact I can't dictate what God should do. It isn't my place to say, "As much as my mom served You, You should've done it this way." No, God is loving and just in all He does. Period.

And in an eye-opening moment for me, the Holy Spirit convicted me that as hard as it was for me to watch my mom die, I needed to remember—and not belittle—how hard it was for God to watch His Son die so my mom, and my redeemed relatives, and my unborn children could live eternally.

Without Christ's defeat of sin and death, none of us would have the assurance of heaven. Thanks to Christ, even in our despair, you and I have victory in Jesus's name.

Think About It: Remember, we do not mourn as those with no hope (1 Thessalonians 4:13). A Christian never experiences spiritual death.

AMBUSHED

Fear the L*ORD and turn away from evil.*
It will be healing to your body and refreshment to your bones.

PROVERBS 3:7-8

Instigating inside fighting has been a warfare tactic of Satan's since the days of Eden. Somewhere in the timespan between Genesis 1 and 3, Satan turned against God and convinced one-third of the angelic host to rebel with him (Revelation 12:4). Then, in Genesis 3, Satan persuaded Adam and Eve to defy God and ignore both His created order for marriage and His command for life on earth.

Next, brother turned against brother when Cain killed Abel. And today, it's not only nation against nation, but Satan is actively working to destroy unity in our homes and churches and communities with infighting. And much of the time, the fighting starts with someone's senseless or hateful words.

The book of Proverbs couldn't be clearer about the dangers of a careless tongue:

- "With the mouth of the foolish, ruin is at hand" (10:14).
- "With his mouth the godless person destroys his

neighbor…By the mouth of the wicked, [a city] is torn down" (11:9, 11).

- "A fool's lips bring strife…His lips are the snare of his soul" (18:6-7).

Proverbs 12:6 even states that "the words of the wicked wait in ambush for blood." And 2 Timothy 2:16-17 adds, "Avoid godless chatter, because those who indulge in it will become more and more ungodly. Their teaching will spread like gangrene" (NIV).

"Hold up," you say. "I'll admit my words are foolish sometimes, but wicked? Godless? Really?"

That's how the Lord sees it.

To guard against infection and ambushes from within, let it begin with you and your circle of friends. Avoid instigating. Speak in ways that uplift others. And when you must address the truth, do it responsibly. James 3:2 affirms, "If anyone does not stumble in what he says, he is a mature man who is also able to control his whole body" (HCSB). In other words, the one who controls their tongue tends to be safe in every way.

Think About It: Spread the gospel rather than the gossip. Make your *faith* contagious, not contentious.

49

NOT AN INCH

With [the tongue] we bless our Lord and Father, and with it we curse people who are made in the likeness of God. From the same mouth come blessing and cursing. My brothers, these things ought not to be so.

JAMES 3:9-10 ESV

As carefully as we need to watch our words around nonbelievers for the sake of our witness, let's be mindful toward our fellow believers as well. Hundreds of times across the Old and New Testaments, Christians are instructed on how to treat and talk to each other within God's family. We're shown how to confront sin directly, when to speak and when to hold our tongue, and more. But not one time is there ever a situation that warrants talking ugly behind another Christian's back.

Matter of fact, the sniping and backstabbing can set back the kingdom of God much like Americans were cautioned in a World War II information manual featured in a National Archives online exhibit. The manual said, "Words are ammunition. Each word an American utters either helps or hurts the war effort. He must stop rumors...He must not speak recklessly. He must remember that the enemy is listening."[5]

Just replace "an American" with "a Christian" in that excerpt, and suddenly it's no longer a call to patriotism but a call to biblical obedience as sons and daughters of God.

Paul warned that when we do not guard our lips and handle our emotions, especially our anger, we are giving the devil an opportunity (Ephesians 4:26-27). The late, great Chicago Bears running back Gale Sayers once said, "Give me 18 inches of daylight. That's all I need." If Sayers's linemen could open up a small hole in the defense, the Hall of Famer was so agile, he could slip through it for a big gain.

Satan doesn't even need 18 inches! He stands outside the doors of churches and Christian homes everywhere, listening. Every bitter word we say, and every scrap we feed the small-group rumor mill, cracks open those doors. Soon enough, he will slip inside and start wreaking havoc in our relationships.

Don't give him a word, people. Not an inch of opportunity. No more talking ugly within the family.

Think About It: Our words can either aid or hurt the enemy's efforts. Let's not aid him. Let's hurt him.

50

LAST MAN STANDING?

At the time of the offering of the evening sacrifice, Elijah the prophet approached and said, "Lord, God of Abraham, Isaac, and Israel, today let it be known that You are God in Israel and that I am Your servant, and that I have done all these things at Your word."

1 KINGS 18:36

In a momentous showdown on Mount Carmel, the prophet Elijah, representing the one true God, had just humiliated and killed the prophets of Baal after proving their god to be a huge fake (1 Kings 18). You'd think he would've been flying high and celebrating God's very public victory. Instead, 1 Kings 19 reports that, under threat of Queen Jezebel, Elijah went on the run, afraid for his life. And once he reached the wilderness, he sat down under a tree and asked the Lord to take his life.

God provided practically for His exhausted servant, giving Elijah rest, food, and water for the next leg of his journey to Mount Horeb. At Horeb weeks later, the Lord asked an interesting question: "What are you doing here, Elijah?" (1 Kings 19:9).

Elijah responded, "I have been very zealous for the Lord, the God of armies; for the sons of Israel have abandoned Your covenant, torn down Your altars, and killed Your prophets with the sword. And I alone am left; and they have sought to take my life" (verse 10). God's response was to pass by Elijah, reminding His servant of His presence through a gentle breeze. Then God asked again, "What are you doing here, Elijah?" (verse 13). The prophet's answer was exactly the same: "I have been very zealous for the LORD…And I alone am left" (verse 14).

Do you get the sense that Elijah was throwing his own pity party? Knowing I can get like this sometimes—not registering all that God is doing on my behalf—I appreciate the Lord's patience toward Elijah. This time, He informed the weary prophet that he was not and would not be alone: God had already prepared a helper and protégé in Elisha (verse 16). What's more, He had counted heads, and there were still seven thousand in Israel who had not bowed to Baal (verse 18).

The next time you think you're the last one standing, take that assumption to the Lord. He'll give you the true picture. And I can guarantee you'll find He *is* providing: practically, spiritually with His presence, and relationally with reinforcements. Look around. He's got you.

> **Think About It:** Our feelings in hard times can be a blindfold to the truth. Don't permit your circumstances to blind you to the truth, but rather to push you to it: You are never alone.

51

HIS STRONG ARM

You have a strong arm; Your hand is mighty, Your right hand is exalted...In Your name [Your people] rejoice all the day...You are the glory of their strength.

PSALM 89:13, 16-17

The game of football wasn't invented until the late 1800s, but when I read about the Lord's undefeated record in Scripture, I can't help but view Him as the ultimate Quarterback: a fearless leader who sees the entire field, calls all the right plays under pressure, and has a strong, accurate arm. These traits equate to someone who can score in any situation and conquer any opponent.

In the Bible, we see Him methodically marching His team to victory, as He did with the Israelites and their seven laps around the city of Jericho. Then, just as effectively, He threw the length of the field to win games with miracle plays, like when He made the sun and moon stand still for an entire day to deliver the Amorites into the hands of Joshua and the army of Israel (Joshua 10).

God's people have always relied on His strong arm to ensure victory. They've always gained confidence from knowing He was leading the charge, just like a great quarterback should. His countless feats include rescuing Israel from Egypt and winning the promised land: "Who is like You, mighty LORD?… You Yourself crushed [Egypt]…You scattered Your enemies with Your mighty arm" (Psalm 89:8, 10); "You with Your own hand drove out the nations…By their own sword [Your people] did not possess the land, and their own arm did not save them, but Your right hand and Your arm and the light of Your presence" (Psalm 44:2-3).

Sometimes you and I will be able to say with biblical warriors like David that "it is God who arms me with strength and keeps my way secure…You armed me with strength for battle" (2 Samuel 22:33, 40 NIV). Other times, He will take matters into His hands and deliver you all by Himself. At all times, He is the centerpiece and the Most Valuable Player.

Look to Him when the enemy is threatening to overtake you. Look to Him when you are under siege. We serve a God who loves to prove Himself strong for His people. Your victory will be won by His strong arm.

Think About It: With this Quarterback on your side, there's no need to take the game into your hands. Give your situation to Him. He will lead you perfectly into the end zone for the score.

52

SHIELD YOURSELF

The Lord takes pleasure in his people; he adorns the humble with salvation. Let the godly exult in glory; let them sing for joy on their beds.

PSALM 149:4-5 ESV

Let's face it. The evil one is hell-bent on amassing as many casualties of war as he can. That's why he is constantly shooting flaming arrows at us—in case he can get past our shield of faith (Ephesians 6:16).

That shield isn't the kind that simply fits over a defender's arm, like Captain America's. The soldier's shield in biblical times went around and over the top of him, for protection from nearly every angle.

What *can* incapacitate even a well-protected soldier, however, is a self-inflicted wound. Willful sins, addictions, compromise, unforgiveness—these are all things Christians have been known to do to themselves. But one of the most common self-inflicted wounds is possibly something you don't even think about: the words you speak over yourself or your circumstances.

It's hard enough to be around somebody who habitually criticizes others, but are you doing that to *yourself*? Are you forecasting gloom and doom as if God isn't in control? If you're saying things like—

"I'm such an idiot."

"Why can't I ever do things right the first time?"

"Just wait: I'll be the one to mess it up."

"Story of my life: the worst that can happen, *will* happen."

—then it probably won't be long before you find yourself limping or laid up, defeated by your own words.

That's not a condemnation. I understand that many people have grown up in homes where these things were said *to* you, and now you say them to yourself. But understand this: God desires truth in our innermost being (Psalm 51:6), and the truth is, God delights in and watches over the ones He loves. So ask the Holy Spirit to renew your mind and empower you to take your thoughts captive so your own tongue doesn't put you in triage. And I pray for you like Paul prayed for the Ephesians: that you would be strengthened *from within* "with power through [God's] spirit in your inner being...to comprehend... the breadth and length and height and depth...[of] the love of Christ." Rather than wounding words, may you "be filled with all the fullness of God," starting today (Ephesians 3:16, 18-19 ESV).

Think About It: While you were a sinner, Christ died for you. That means, even at your worst, He loved you and considered you worth the sacrifice.

53

GOOD TO GO

The LORD said to [Jeremiah], "Do not say, 'I am a youth,' because everywhere I send you, you shall go, and all that I command you, you shall speak. Do not be afraid of them, for I am with you to save you."

JEREMIAH 1:7-8

For someone who ended up being such a powerful leader of God's people, Moses was full of excuses when God first called him: "Who am I, that I should go to Pharaoh, and that I should bring the sons of Israel out of Egypt?" (Exodus 3:11). "What if they ask who sent me? What should I say?" (verse 13, paraphrased). "What if they will not believe me or listen to what I say?" (Exodus 4:1).

God answered:

"Assuredly I will be with you" (3:12).

"Tell the sons of Israel: 'I AM has sent me to you'" (see verse 14).

"Here are miraculous signs from Me" (see 4:2-9).

Then Moses tried: "Please, Lord, I have never been eloquent...for I am slow of speech" (Exodus 4:10), and he pressed the issue until God angrily appointed Moses's brother to accompany him as a mouthpiece. Still, the Lord wanted His servant to hear loud and clear that even a silver tongue like Aaron's would not be sufficient, reiterating, "*I Myself* will be with your mouth and his mouth, and I will instruct you in what you are to do" (verse 15). The Lord would be Moses's Help and Provider in this new role.

In which assignment are you pushing back at God with one excuse after another? My dad, Tony Evans, wrote a devotional book years ago titled *No More Excuses*. Let that be your constant motto in your relationship with God: that you will offer Him no more excuses, but rather your ears, as young Samuel did—"Speak, for Your servant is listening" (1 Samuel 3:10).

You may be a youth like the prophet Jeremiah, old like Elizabeth, or small like David. You may have a past like Paul's, where you previously set yourself against God, or be from a small family (or town) like Gideon that no one expects anything of. Never mind what you perceive as your disadvantages or disqualifiers. If, by His Spirit, our mighty God is instructing you to "go and do," then you're good to go in His name. You'll have everything you need to follow where He leads and glorify Him. Most of all, you'll have *Him.* Do not be afraid.

Think About It: Like Moses, you are saying, "Am I?" and God is responding, "No, you're not, but I Am. So go!"

54

KEEP GROWING

We do not lose heart, but though our outer person is decaying, yet our inner person is being renewed day by day.

2 CORINTHIANS 4:16

"Our outer person is decaying." Can you relate to that description? As the years pile on, your knees start popping; your neck hurts because you slept wrong; you can't eat all those spicy foods like you used to; you get winded a whole lot faster; you sneeze and think you cracked your ribs...That's why I'm glad God assures us that our inner person—what is eternal about us—can continue to increase and gain strength until our final breath, when *everything* about us will be thoroughly renewed and made whole.

To keep your inner person growing and revitalized, try these simple exercises. They will be health to your soul:

Do something for your spiritual, emotional, and physical health every day. Romans 8:6 says, "The mind set on the Spirit is life and peace." Verse 10 adds: "If Christ is in you...the spirit is alive because of righteousness." His Spirit will give life to your mortal body. Giving consistent attention to these areas is as essential as hydrating regularly during a workout.

Be sure to include "Encourage someone else" in your daily activities.

Second Corinthians 1:3-4 reminds us that "the Father of mercies and God of all comfort, who comforts us in all our affliction," equips His family for the powerful ministry of offering to others what we have received from Him. You will be especially strengthened as you look to strengthen others.

Invite other believers to come alongside you. The devil loves to turn isolation into desolation. God, however, sustains and often provides for us directly through our spiritual brothers and sisters. If you need something today, say so. Communicate with your pastor or small-group leader. And if you haven't already, join a church and small group to ensure that people are walking with you through life.

Make anything a cause for thanks. Nothing is too insignificant, because *every* good gift comes from our Father in heaven (James 1:17).

There's no limit to how much our faith can grow. Isn't that great news? Though life's battles will weaken and weary us physically, every believer can claim—and experience—the victorious words of Hebrews 10:39: "We are not among those who shrink back to destruction, but of those who have faith for the safekeeping of the soul."

Think About It: Simply put, you can be older and younger at the same time. It just takes some spiritual exercise.

55

BOAST IN WHAT?

We are the true circumcision, who worship in the Spirit of God and take pride in Christ Jesus, and put no confidence in the flesh.

PHILIPPIANS 3:3

As a follow-up to the previous reading, here's another thing you can do to keep growing inwardly, regardless of what's going on physically or in your circumstances: *Boast in your weaknesses.* I mean it! Do this anytime you feel frustration or discouragement seeping in.

When the apostle Paul pled for the Lord to remove a tormenting thorn in the flesh, God didn't take it away. Rather, He answered, "My grace is sufficient for you, for [My] power is perfected in weakness." To which Paul responded, "I will rather boast about my weaknesses, so that the power of Christ may dwell in me...for when I am weak, then I am strong" (2 Corinthians 12:9-10).

In admitting how helpless he was to fix his situation, Paul's sufferings effectively diminished his self-confidence. But did you notice what came of it? He grew all the more Christ-confident. His weakened self-confidence opened the way for the power of Christ to take over, just as an electrical outage from a storm gives one of those fancy home generators the opportunity to show how well it can light up a house and supply its occupants with energy.

I challenge you, warrior, to boast in your weaknesses as they become apparent to you in your battles:

"Thank You, God, that I can't do this on my own."

"Lord, show me the next step, because I have no clue what You have in mind."

"I'm relying on You in my pain…confusion…fear…anger. You are my Help."

Though it won't feel like it at first, every time you lose some of your own strength, you receive double; you gain more of Christ, and His strength becomes even more obvious in you. As you depend on Jesus, the more you will realize, like Paul did, "the surpassing value of knowing Christ Jesus [the] Lord…and the power of His resurrection" (Philippians 3:8, 10). Believer, boast in Him!

Think About It: Growing up from childhood to adulthood in the world is about independence. Growing up from childhood to adulthood in spiritual maturity is about dependence. We must not confuse the two.

56

WALKING WOUNDED

Brothers and sisters, since we have confidence to enter the holy place by the blood of Jesus...and since we have a great priest over the house of God, let's approach God with a sincere heart in full assurance of faith, having our hearts sprinkled clean from an evil conscience and our bodies washed with pure water.

HEBREWS 10:19, 21-22

Legendary UCLA men's basketball coach John Wooden was often known to say, "There is no pillow as soft as a clean conscience." That kind of peace is every Christian's dream. Yet if we're not careful, Satan can pierce us with the arrows of current or past sin. The ones that cause us to say, "I just can't forgive myself," even though we've been promised that Jesus saves *completely* anyone who comes to God through Him (Hebrews 7:24-25).

My question is: Have you received God's forgiveness?

"Oh yeah, I'm saved," you say.

But that's not what I asked. I asked if you've *received* His forgiveness.

I'm asking because believing and receiving are not the same thing. You see, God always stands ready to extend relationship-restoring forgiveness to His sons and daughters. He will dispense it anytime, any day. Yet lots of Christians don't take Him up on the offer. You know how it is—many of us refuse to go to the doctor, or we refuse to take the medicine our doctor prescribes. We'll risk infection instead, too afraid to ask or too ashamed to be seen.

But let me urge you to have the attitude of the woman who'd been bleeding for 12 years. She was sure Jesus would heal her if she could just touch the hem of His robe. True enough, as soon as she reached out to Him, Jesus turned and saw her and said, "'Have courage, daughter... Your faith has made you well.' And the woman was made well from that moment" (Matthew 9:22 HCSB).

A clear conscience comes not only from believing in Christ for salvation, but in receiving His forgiveness as often as you need it. Once you receive it, the healing will start to set in. You'll no longer have the pain of distancing yourself from Jesus or the guilt the enemy was using to pierce your soul.

Go see Jesus in the infirmary, will you? Show Jesus your wounds. With compassion He will say to you, "Have courage, child." Your faith, combined with His forgiveness, will make you well.

Think About It: If you're one of the walking wounded, there's no better time than the present to take your wounds to Christ and let Him personally assure you, "I died for that. My blood covered it. See? I have the scars in My hands and feet to prove it."

57

IT'S PERSONAL

The L*ORD* *God is a sun and shield; the* L*ORD* *gives grace and glory; He withholds no good thing from those who walk with integrity.*

PSALM 84:11

There's no denying that God is utterly holy and righteous, and He deserves reverence in all things. But He tenderly cares for you too. In fact, He loves you so much that it's personal! Like the Israelites in the Old Testament, you can make Him proud, glad, jealous—or even sad. Psalm 78:40-41 reports that their regular rebellions "grieved" and "pained the Holy One of Israel." Doesn't that put things in a different light, knowing your responses to Him matter that much?

I get how life's disappointments or difficulties can make us wary of Him. Yet those are the times we need to run *to* God. If you could use a touch from Him today, ask Him to encourage you. To reveal His love to you personally through His Word and the work of His Spirit. Also, copy down these biblical passages that express His heart toward His loved ones. He cares for you in the same ways.

- "Jerusalem, Jerusalem...How often I wanted to gather

your children together, the way a hen gathers her chicks under her wings" (Matthew 23:37).

- "The steps of a man are established by the LORD, and He delights in his way" (Psalm 37:23).
- "How precious also are Your thoughts for me, God! How vast is the sum of them! Were I to count them, they would outnumber the sand" (Psalm 139:17-18).
- "Comfort, comfort My people…Speak kindly to Jerusalem; and call out to her, that her warfare has ended, that her guilt has been removed" (Isaiah 40:1-2).
- "Thus says the LORD.., he who formed you, O Israel: 'Fear not, for I have redeemed you; I have called you by name, you are mine'" (Isaiah 43:1 ESV).
- "The LORD is my shepherd, I lack nothing. He makes me lie down in green pastures, he leads me beside quiet waters, he refreshes my soul" (Psalm 23:1-3 NIV).
- "The LORD your God…will rejoice over you with gladness, He will quiet you with His love, He will rejoice over you with singing" (Zephaniah 3:17 NKJV).

Think About It: All through Scripture, God wants you to know He cares for you. Now it's on you to believe it.

58

RESOLUTE

Let us throw off everything that hinders and the sin that so easily entangles. And let us run with perseverance the race marked out for us, fixing our eyes on Jesus, the pioneer and perfecter of faith...Consider him who endured such opposition from sinners, so that you will not grow weary and lose heart.

HEBREWS 12:1-3 NIV

For decades, the marathon has been the final event of the Summer Olympics. These world-class athletes work hard to arrive at the Games in peak condition, yet there are always some who start the race but never make it to the end. Beside those disappointed runners' names, race officials assign the letters *DNF*, for *Did Not Finish*, in the final results.

Thinking of those men and women reminds me of what Jesus endured during the last hours of His earthly race. Especially as I recall the challenges that stood in the way of Him completing what He'd started: The rejection and betrayal by His closest friends. The injustice of His death sentence. Public humiliation. The beating, thirst, and physical agony. And worst of all, the silence of His Father in heaven while Jesus bore the weight of our sins.

He could have let any of those things take Him out. At any point, He could've said, "I'm done. I'm not going through with this." Instead, He is the only one in history to ever be able to say He triumphed completely undefeated, failing at nothing He was given to do (John 17:4).

What was His mindset? As the days drew near for Him to be taken up to heaven, "he set his face to go to Jerusalem," where He knew these sufferings awaited Him (Luke 9:51 ESV). The NIV Bible translates the original Greek as: "Jesus resolutely set out for Jerusalem."

Our Savior *set his face*. He fixed His eyes. By the power of heaven, and out of love for His Father and for us, He would not be deterred.

Jesus our Forerunner ran such a textbook race that none of us ever has to question whether we will be able to complete ours. Whether you're at mile marker 26 or you're just getting started, He can coach you on how to stay the course and overcome *your* obstacles. Read up on how He did it in the Gospels of Matthew, Mark, Luke, and John. Then follow after Him so you can run resolutely to the finish and celebrate the victory.

Think About It: Start with the attitude of Christ when He said, "Not My will, but Yours be done" (Luke 22:42). A strong start can propel you to a stronger finish.

59

WHETHER BY LIFE OR BY DEATH

I will not be put to shame in anything, but that with all boldness, Christ will even now, as always, be exalted in my body, whether by life or by death.

PHILIPPIANS 1:20

At my mom's funeral, my sister Priscilla shared a story from about six weeks earlier, when Mom burst into tears while scrolling through Facebook. Some of my family members, including Priscilla, rushed to her side, asking, "Why are you crying?"

"I'm crying," Mom said, "because I'm reading the prayers of all these people in our church, and so many other churches, in continents and countries around the world, asking God to heal me—and what will happen to their faith if God doesn't answer the way they're praying?"

She didn't want anyone's faith to waver on her account. She didn't want anyone to think, *See? God isn't who He says He is. He's powerless to do what He says He can do.* Because her own faith remained steadfast to the very end.

What was Lois Evans's secret? From the first day of her diagnosis until God ushered her home, she was confident that God cannot and does not lie (Titus 1:2)—so she was able to say to her dying day, "I know that this will turn out for my deliverance through your prayers and the provision of the Spirit of Jesus Christ" (Philippians 1:19).

None of us knows how God will answer in our times of adversity, but we can learn to trust His answer. If you're not there yet, don't despair. No one develops a rooted, no-matter-what-comes faith overnight. Not even Jesus's closest disciples. But like the sick boy's father did in Mark 9:24, you can bring your seed of faith to Jesus and ask Him to grow it, praying, "I do believe; help my unbelief!"

Think About It: My mom would want me to tell you, "Don't lose faith. Because no matter what God's answer is, the outcome is victory."

60

READY FOR ACTION

Prepare your minds for action, keep sober in spirit, set your hope completely on the grace to be brought to you at the revelation of Jesus Christ.

1 PETER 1:13

From ancient times a decline in courage has been considered the beginning of the end." That's what Nobel Prize winner and political prisoner Aleksandr Solzhenitsyn warned Harvard graduates in a commencement address years ago.

Courage isn't easy to come by. Especially in times like ours, when people of faith are battling increasing opposition from all sides: our culture, our classrooms, the media, even sometimes from the person sitting beside us in the pew. Jesus told us to expect it: "If they persecuted Me, they will persecute you as well" (John 15:20). He spoke of not *if* but "*when* the people hate you, and when they exclude you, and insult you, and scorn your name as evil, on account of the Son of Man" (Luke 6:22). Paul wrote, "Everyone who wants to live a godly life in Christ Jesus will be persecuted" (2 Timothy 3:12 NIV). And the pressure is only going to ramp up as Christ's return draws nearer. Paul warned that in the last days, people will be arrogant, malicious, treacherous, reckless, brutal, and haters of good and of God (2 Timothy 3:1-4).

In the face of all that, fewer people will have courage. Fewer will elect to stand up for what is righteous and true. But that's what being committed to the cause of Christ requires. You've been called to active duty, not passive duty. You've been forewarned so you can prepare your mind for action and take proper action when the time for action comes.

It sounds like Civil War colonel Joshua Chamberlain was prepared in just that way when his moment of decision came. History records that at the Battle of Gettysburg, the scholarly Chamberlain, who had not only attended seminary but pored over every military book and manual he could find, decided to attack the Confederate army with bayonets rather than retreating, even though his men were vastly outnumbered and out of ammunition. The strategy proved successful, and his decision delivered a Union victory in one of the Civil War's most crucial battles.

What was the colonel's take on that moment afterward? Simply this: "I had deep within me the inability to do nothing." I pray God gives each of us that same resolve when our day of opposition comes.

Think About It: You can't overcome without opposition. Victory means there is a battle somewhere. Therefore, to experience victory, we must fight the battle.

61

FOLLOW THROUGH

Not everyone who says to Me, "Lord, Lord," will enter the kingdom of heaven, but the one who does the will of My Father who is in heaven will enter.

MATTHEW 7:21

As a former athlete and now as a sports chaplain, I can tell you one thing for certain: Talk is cheap. Anybody with a mouth can claim what they will do come game time. What matters is what you do once game time comes.

Soldiering is similar. Nobody in your unit cares what your combat-video avatar can do. Unless you finish boot camp and prove yourself in the line of duty, you're just full of hot air.

Actions are the evidence. They reveal what you truly believe and whose side you're really on.

John the Apostle framed the marks of a Christian like this: "By this we know that we have come to know [God], if we keep His commandments. The one who says, 'I have come to know Him,' and does not keep His commandments, is a liar, and the truth is not in him" (1 John 2:3-4). And in the next chapter: "Make sure no one deceives you; the one who practices righteousness is righteous, just as [Christ] is righteous; the one who practices sin is of the devil...By this the children of God and the children of the devil are obvious" (3:7-8, 10).

Brag all you want that you're on God's side; call Him "Lord" and pray long, eloquent prayers like the Pharisees did. He won't be fooled. "The Lord knows those who are His" (2 Timothy 2:19). He knows His sheep, His players, His soldiers, His family. Not by their words but by their follow-through. And He's got no time for liars.

Jesus verified that at the final judgment, the ones who will inherit the kingdom are those who, during their time on earth, put their words to work: feeding the hungry, inviting the stranger in, clothing the naked, comforting the sick, visiting the prisoner—all in the name of Christ and out of devotion to Him (Matthew 25:34-36).

Talk is about as easy as it comes, but God looks beyond the chatter and noise, watching for who follows through on their faith in Christ. God knows who really believes in His Son (John 6:40) and who is faking it. John said it well: "Let's not love with word or with tongue, but in deed and truth" (1 John 3:18).

Think About It: It's easy to know what someone believes by just watching them. What do people think you believe by watching you?

62

WHITEWASHED

It is not the one who commends himself that is approved, but the one whom the Lord commends.

2 CORINTHIANS 10:18

For those of you who have been to Long Beach Harbor in California, you know you can't miss it: One of Great Britain's most famous modern-era passenger ships, the *Queen Mary*, has been permanently moored there since the late 1960s.

When it was launched in 1936, *Mary* was the largest ocean liner ever, and considerably bigger than the *Titanic*. She served through three decades and a world war until she was retired and converted into a floating hotel and museum.

During the conversion process from sailing ship to tourist attraction, *Mary*'s enormous smokestacks disintegrated. Once engineers got past the surface, they discovered that practically all the original steel inside the stacks was gone, eaten away by rust. What remained were several years' worth of paint jobs. The identifying feature of this legendary ship was little more than three decayed shells being held together by a couple dozen layers of paint.

Doesn't that remind you of those self-proclaimed Christians who act all righteous and religious but in reality are fakers and hypocrites? Satan has been using infiltrators like them to undermine the church since its earliest days. Jesus called out the ones in *His* day, saying, "You are like whitewashed tombs which on the outside appear beautiful, but inside they are full of dead men's bones and all uncleanness. So you, too, outwardly appear righteous to people, but inwardly you are full of hypocrisy and lawlessness" (Matthew 23:27-28).

While we need to be on the lookout for those among us who uphold double standards or self-righteously distort Scripture, it's just as important that we protect ourselves from their smugness and hypocrisy. How? "Be diligent to present yourself *approved to God* [not to yourself] as a worker…accurately handling the word of truth" (2 Timothy 2:15). Study the sacred writings of Scripture like your life depends on it—because those truths *are* "able to make you wise for salvation through faith in Christ Jesus" (2 Timothy 3:15 NIV). And whenever God's Word teaches you, reproves you, or corrects you, don't resist it. Be thankful, for you are being trained in true righteousness, that you "may be thoroughly equipped for every good work" (2 Timothy 3:17 NIV).

Think About It: Are there areas in your life where you are being hypocritical? Don't just watch out for the hypocrisy of others. Use God's Word to watch out for yourself.

HERO? NO!

[The Israelites] will cry out to the LORD because of oppressors, and He will send them a Savior and a Champion.

ISAIAH 19:20

When the Philistine fighting machine, Goliath, stepped out in front of his army and shouted at the men of Israel across the Valley of Elah, "Choose a man as your representative and have him come down to me" for a one-on-one fight (1 Samuel 17:8), he was calling for an ancient-era type of duel known as "single combat" or "champion warfare." Two individual warriors representing their respective armies would battle each other on neutral ground while their fellow soldiers watched. The outcome of this fight would decide the winner and loser of the conflict between the opposing armies.

Three times in 1 Samuel 17, Goliath is referred to as the Philistine "champion" (verses 4, 23, 51). He wore the title so convincingly that even Saul, Israel's king, wouldn't take him on. The army of Israel and its leader cowered on their side of the valley, believing they had no one to battle for them.

Enter David, who volunteered to fight this "uncircumcised Philistine" (verse 26). To use Bible commentator Matthew Poole's description, this so-called champion—someone who was outside the covenant—was both "a stranger and enemy to God."[6] That fact alone let the lowly shepherd know he had the advantage, because David was neither a stranger nor an enemy of the one true God. Look at how boldly he answered the opponent for everyone to hear: "I come to you in the name of the LORD of armies, the God of the armies of Israel, whom you have defied. This day the LORD will hand you over to me...that this entire assembly may know that the LORD does not save by sword or by spear; for the battle is the LORD's, and He will hand you over to us!" (verses 45-47).

Six times in these two statements alone, David refers to the Lord as the One who will be central to the victory. Israel already had a champion. David was only a representative. He didn't have to be the hero.

After David scored a biblical knockout with just one stone to the giant's head, Saul and the people of Israel celebrated David as their champion in this battle, but David knew better. The real Champion of Israel was God Himself.

Isn't it great to know that anytime you're facing a giant, you don't have to be the hero either? Those battles of *yours* belong to the Lord. Let the Champion do the fighting for you.

Think About It: Do you look at the battle through the context of your belief, or does your belief shrink when you face big battles?

64

A STRONG FOUNDATION

Every house is built by someone, but the builder of all things is God.

HEBREWS 3:4 ESV

Once you've experienced a weak foundation of any kind, you can appreciate how important a strong one is.

Have you ever lived in a house with a poorly laid foundation? The large cracks at ground level are the telltale signs of instability. And unless the problem is remedied, the weakness below is going to work its way up to whatever stands above it. With a house, for example, you go from seeing cracks in the concrete, to walking on uneven floors, to doors that won't close properly. Eventually, the walls start showing cracks too.

Our lives and relationships are just like that. You've experienced this if you had to work doubly hard as an adult to compensate for the gaps in your education. Or you had to dig out some of the religious notions you were taught as a child. Or you grew up with a parent whose moods or rules constantly shifted, and now you hesitate about having kids of your own, unsure what kind of parent you'll be.

This is the reason Satan so often targets our spiritual and

relational foundations first: Our enemy knows a house divided, literally or figuratively, will not stand (Mark 3:25). So to destroy a culture, he will start by destabilizing marriages and eroding family values. To destroy a church, he will introduce subtle shifts in doctrine or slowly reposition people's hearts from a spirit of unity and prayer toward a spirit of division and self-interest.

Thankfully, you never have to settle for the foundations you've inherited. You can make changes in *your* marriage, in how you raise *your* kids, in *your* relationship with God. You can improve on *your* knowledge of Scripture. Ask other builders whose work you admire to show you how they did it. The Lord will be right there beside you too, sleeves rolled up, helping you shore up your existing foundations—or helping you build new and better. Helping you build on the Rock, not on shifting sand. After all, your life is His house. He's invested in making sure *yours* lasts as a dwelling for future generations.

Which foundations of yours need attention? Do an inspection with the Master Architect and Builder of the universe. Whatever He finds, He can fix.

Think About It: The Lord knows everything there is to know about establishing a foundation that can withstand life's storms (Matthew 7:24-27). Don't put things off another day. Call in the Expert, and let the work begin!

THE DECIDING FACTOR

We keep the charge of the LORD our God,
but you have forsaken him.

2 CHRONICLES 13:11 ESV

At one point in Israel's history after King Solomon died, its 12 tribes divided into two kingdoms. In 2 Chronicles 13, those kingdoms are about to do battle. Here's the scene:

Abijah is king of Judah, Israel's northern kingdom (consisting of only the tribes of Benjamin and Judah), with an army of 400,000 men. Jeroboam rules Israel's southern kingdom, the other ten tribes, and he has brought 800,000 warriors to the battle line (verse 3).

Though outnumbered two to one, Abijah openly claims victory *ahead of the victory* for one reason: He and his people have not forsaken the Lord like their brethren in the southern kingdom have. Judah's king confidently adds, "Behold, God is with us at our head," before delivering this final warning: "Sons of Israel, do not fight against the LORD God of your fathers, for you will not succeed" (verse 12).

Jeroboam is unswayed. After all, he has the numbers to terrify Abijah's army from the front, *plus* he has set up an ambush to surprise them from behind. Upon realizing they are hemmed in, Judah cries out to the Lord, and "God defeated Jeroboam and all Israel" (verse 15). *God* did it. With enemy troops at Judah's front and rear.

What was the deciding factor? Did God love the northern kingdom more than the southern kingdom? No, this was a war between His people, with kin fighting kin. Choosing favorites would've been like Peyton and Eli Manning's dad, Archie, rooting for one son over another whenever the two brothers' teams faced off during their NFL careers. Good fathers don't do that. Instead, the Bible explains that the men of Judah "conquered because *they trusted in the Lord*" (verse 18).

Verses 14-15 indicate their war cry wasn't the customary attempt to intimidate the enemy. (That wouldn't have worked this time anyway.) Rather, Judah's war cry was a shout *to the Lord.* Even as their situation worsened from being outnumbered to being surrounded, their faith and hope remained in God alone.

Abijah's pro tip? Side with God.

Think About It: Is the enemy closing in on your life? Have you been ambushed *and* outnumbered? The deciding factor in your battle is the same: You can either follow God or forsake God.

66

ADVANTAGE: GOD

Who is God besides the Lord? And who is the Rock except our God? It is God who arms me with strength and keeps my way secure.

2 SAMUEL 22:32-33 NIV

Though the warring parties are different, the deciding factor in the battle account of 1 Chronicles 5 is the same as what we read in 2 Chronicles 13. God fought for the Reubenites, the Gadites, and the half-tribe of Manasseh as they faced a faction of Ishmaelites. The chronicler reports, "God delivered the Hagrites and all their allies into their hands, because they cried out to him during the battle. He answered their prayers, because they trusted in him." They saw victory "because the battle was God's" (1 Chronicles 5:20, 22 NIV).

What's noteworthy about the 1 Chronicles 5 battle is, the odds weren't against these guys from Israel. Whereas Abijah's army was massively outnumbered, the nearly 45,000 men from the three tribes within Israel had the upper hand. The Bible specifies they were "ready for military service" (verse 18 NIV). The fact that this is mentioned tells us they were *really* ready. Warriors in every sense of the word. These were "able-bodied men who could handle shield and sword, who could use a bow, and who were trained for battle" (verse 18 NIV). The ESV Bible describes them as "expert in war" (verse 18). If ever an army was fit, equipped, trained, and capable of defeating its foe, it was them. Nevertheless, they depended on God.

Read the chapter for yourself. Their war cry, their prayers, their quest for victory—everything was centered on Him instead of themselves. For all they were bringing to the battle, they were focused on what *the Lord* was bringing to their battle.

This is important for us to understand, because in life, we aren't always the underdogs. By worldly standards, you may often have the background, the training, the confidence, and the know-how to win. Still, the reason for God-reliance doesn't change: *He is God, and we are not.*

Pastor John Piper has said, "God is not looking for people to work for Him, so much as He is looking for people who will let Him work for them."[7] Whether or not we appear to have the advantage, the Almighty God *is* our advantage.

Think About It: God has called us to be stewards of the battle, not owners. Your job is to be the best steward you can be, but to let God own your battle.

WORRY ABOUT *YOU*

As for us, the LORD is our God,
and we have not forsaken him.

2 CHRONICLES 13:10 ESV

Man, does it ever hurt when people you know and love declare war against you! You're on the side of right, yet they're wronging you.

Those are the times you want to go after them the way they're going after you. Get them back, or, at the very least, call them out to God: "Lord, look at everything they're doing! You need to punish them!"

However, something I've noticed about God is that He doesn't need our input about what to do. Not even a little. Nobody is pulling one over on Him. He's been watching the play-by-play. And most importantly, He sees the hearts of everyone involved.

Why, then, doesn't our obedience to God always result in quick victory, like we often see in the Old Testament especially? I'll bet you can name past circumstances—maybe even your current one—where the victory train was taking forever to arrive at your station. Meanwhile, it seemed like the people lined up against you, who were openly sinning, were winning.

As maddening as times like these are, you can't get hung up on the mystery of God's timing or on what your opponent is up to. Cry out to God if you need to, and call out the sin of your foe if the Holy Spirit compels you...but ultimately, your responsibility is simple: Don't focus on them; focus on you. Worry about *you*.

"As for us, the Lord is our God and we have not forsaken him," is where King Abijah of Judah set his sights as his army went to battle against the idol-worshiping southern kingdom of Israel (2 Chronicles 13:10 esv). That sounds a lot like Joshua. Remember how he challenged all the tribes of Israel after they'd reached the promised land? "Choose for yourselves today whom you will serve...But as for me and my house, we will serve the Lord" (Joshua 24:15).

God is aware of the score, and He won't allow sin to go on forever. So put the enemy's antics in His hands. Let Him handle them. As for you and your house, you concentrate on doing the God thing, okay? For He hasn't forgotten you.

Think About It: Don't forget God's Playbook in your battles. It was written for you to overcome, not for you to be overcome. And remember, your Coach is paying attention to how you play.

68

GO WITH GOD

The Spirit of God came on Azariah...and he went out to meet Asa and said to him, "Listen to me, Asa, and all Judah and Benjamin: the Lord is with you when you are with Him. And if you seek Him, He will let you find Him; but if you abandon Him, He will abandon you."

2 CHRONICLES 15:1-2

After King Abijah died, Asa, his son, assumed the throne. Like his father, Asa relied on the Lord. God rewarded his faithfulness by prospering Judah and giving them years and years of "peace on every side" (2 Chronicles 14:7 ESV). And when Judah did go to war, God delivered an incredible victory over a million-man army nearly twice the size of Asa's army.

One day, the king received a word from the Lord that ended with this promise: "You, be strong and do not lose courage, for there is a reward for your work" (2 Chronicles 15:7).

This fired up Asa even more! He instituted additional religious reforms, including deposing his own mother for making an idol. These efforts sparked spiritual revival across the kingdom, which culminated in a massive worship service in Jerusalem during the fifteenth year of his reign. Many who participated were defectors from the southern kingdom because they saw how clearly the Lord was with Asa. Verse 12 says the people "entered into the covenant to seek the LORD God of their fathers with all their heart and soul." As for their king, verse 17 describes Asa's heart as being "wholly true" (ESV).

Fast-forward 20 years. The king of Israel, Baasha, was jealous that his people kept moving to Judah. His idea was to build a fortified city north of Jerusalem that would stand in their way.

For some reason, when Asa got wind of this, he persuaded (and bribed) the king of Syria to ally with him to protect Judah. It worked. Ben-hadad's armies conquered several of Israel's cities, and Baasha stopped construction. But this decision put Asa under the discipline of the Lord. He had not stayed with God. Therefore, Judah would be embroiled in war.

This just goes to show that our faith commitment is never automatic. It's great that you were close with God last year, last week, or even yesterday, but what about today? Every day, every decision, and every challenge in life calls for a conscious decision to stay devoted. Go with God, will you? As long as you're with God, you're good.

Think About It: As my dad says, "We can't be two-timing God—committed to Him on Sunday and to the world on Monday." In your life with God, *every* day is the Lord's day.

69

DAMAGE CONTROL

The one who wants to love life and to see good days
must keep his tongue from evil and his lips from speaking deceit.

1 PETER 3:10 HCSB

The book of James doesn't hold back about how destructive our words are. First, the tongue is called a *fire* that is "set on fire by hell" (James 3:6).

What does a fire need to start? Just three things: (1) a spark, (2) something to burn, and (3) oxygen. So...not much. A little gossip, one cruel comment, a quick lie, or calling somebody a hateful name is all it takes for our words to ignite, setting on fire the course of someone's life. In no time at all, that tiny spark can become an inferno, especially online—burning up a reputation, a business, a relationship, an entire church, or a person's faith. The damage we are capable of reminds me of the Canadian wildfires of 2023, which were so extensive their pollution affected all of Canada and many regions of the US, including the East Coast, and crossed over the Atlantic into Europe. In other words, the devastation was so vast, its effects cannot be calculated.

James also calls the tongue "a restless evil, full of deadly poison" (verse 8). It is unsettled, unstable, and never satisfied in its depravity. Once it gets going, it's almost impossible to stop. The venom in a rattlesnake bite can kill a person in as little as six hours. Prior to death, that bite causes severe pain; can produce internal bleeding, paralysis, or suffocation; and attacks the heart, the brain, and the nervous system. Emotionally and spiritually, the venom in our words does the same to our victims.

Tragically, we often don't realize the damage we've done to others until someone's words burn us or poison a person we love. Now that you know better, ask the Holy Spirit to help you do better. Next time you realize you've hurt someone with your words, start damage control immediately, like Proverbs 6:3-4 advises: "Go, humble yourself, and plead with your neighbor. Don't give sleep to your eyes or slumber to your eyelids" until you have apologized and tried to make things right (HCSB). Maybe you'll be able to douse the fire while it can still be extinguished.

Think About It: Loving life and seeing good days has a lot to do with what one says. Why? Because by the measure in which you give, it will return to you (Luke 6:38).

70

FROM THE FOXHOLE

My soul waits in silence for God alone;
from Him comes my salvation.
He alone is my rock and my salvation,
my stronghold; I will not be greatly shaken.

PSALM 62:1-2

Ever feel like you're in a foxhole in the middle of a war, with grenades dropping everywhere? I'm pretty sure that's the equivalent of how David felt in Psalm 62:3, when he wrote of his enemies: "How long will you attack a man, that you may murder him, all of you…?" While on the run from Saul, David described in Psalm 57:4: "My soul is among lions; I must lie among those who devour, among sons of mankind whose teeth are spears and arrows, and their tongue is a sharp sword."

In his lifetime, he faced everything from family drama to being targeted by his "boss," King Saul, to multiple murder plots against him. In Psalm 3, when David's own son had gathered an army to overthrow and kill him, David lamented, "LORD, how they have increased who trouble me! Many are they who rise up against me. Many are they who say of me, 'There is no help for him in God'" (verses 1-2 NKJV).

Those were the facts. Many people *were* against him, saying terrible things.

But look at this. Here comes the faith: "But You, O LORD, are a shield for me, my glory and the One who lifts up my head. I cried to the LORD with my voice, and He heard me from His holy hill" (verses 3-4).

David had a habit of looking to heaven from the foxholes. His first four words were a game changer: "But You, O LORD..."

Where would any of us be if not for God?

The facts are: Life in this world is sometimes overwhelming. All kinds of evil forces are throwing grenades and gunning for us (Ephesians 6:12). We would be doomed except for one overriding *Factor*: "But You, O Lord."

Think About It: Do you make it your habit to look to heaven from the foxhole? Your help is in God alone.

71

PERMANENT

[The earth and the heavens] will perish, but You remain;
and they all will wear out like a garment...
But You are the same, and Your years will not come to an end.

HEBREWS 1:11-12

Anytime I hear someone claim that a sports record will never be broken, or that something was "built to last forever," my ears perk up. Just watch one day's worth of any Olympic Games or one episode of a show like *Engineering Catastrophes*. Right away you'll see that nothing of this earth lasts. Somehow, some way, every human endeavor or invention will either fall or fail.

Let me tell you what *will* last. I'll give you a list—and this is just for starters:

- "*His steadfast love* endures forever!" (1 Chronicles 16:34 ESV).
- "*Your dominion* endures throughout all generations" (Psalm 145:13).
- "*The mercy of the LORD* is from everlasting to everlasting for those who fear Him" (Psalm 103:17).

- "*My words* will not pass away" (Matthew 24:35).
- "*His righteousness* endures forever"; "*His faithfulness* is everlasting" (Psalm 111:3; 136:1).
- "*Everything God does* will remain forever" (Ecclesiastes 3:14).
- "*Jesus Christ* is the same yesterday and today, and forever" (Hebrews 13:8).
- "*His kingdom* will have no end" (Luke 1:33).

All of that would be amazing enough. But God goes one step further, making this permanent promise to anybody who puts their faith in Christ: Though "the world is passing away... the one who does the will of God continues to live forever" (1 John 2:17).

How can it happen that fallen, fading people like us can have a forever too? We are loved "with an everlasting love" (Jeremiah 31:3), and Jesus expressed this with the ultimate sacrifice. Praise God for the One who has made the permanence of our salvation, and our future in heaven, possible!

Think About It: Choose the verses from the list above that you need to be reminded of most right now. Then review them until you've committed them to memory.

GO DEEP!

[I pray] that Christ may dwell in your hearts through faith—that you, being rooted and grounded in love, may have strength to comprehend…and to know the love of Christ that surpasses knowledge, that you may be filled with all the fullness of God.

EPHESIANS 3:17-19 ESV

In Ephesians 3, Paul prayed that the believers in Ephesus would be *rooted and grounded, filled and full.* This is maturity. This is what God the Father brings to fruition for His children through faith in Christ and the work of the Holy Spirit.

Let's look at this a little more closely. According to Bible commentators, the words *rooted* and *grounded* express a simple idea: to be deeply fixed and securely settled. Colossians 2:7 speaks of being "firmly rooted and now being built up in [Christ] and established in your faith." Here's what's interesting about the kind of growth being mentioned here.

Matthew Henry observed that "spiritual growth consists most in the growth of the root."[8] Charles Ellicott wrote, "The idea implied in 'rooted' is of the striking down deeper and spreading wider into the soil."[9] He adds that while we typically think of growing upward, "here that growth is downward, deeper and deeper into the communion with God in Christ."[10]

What happens then? As God's people grow deep and strong at the root in their love for Christ, they are able to stand tall, no matter what storms may come.

If you're not seeing as much fruit or foliage in your relationship with God as you'd like, or you sense you are weak at the roots, let me suggest something on a practical level: Instead of going wider—adding more spiritual disciplines—go deeper. Start using a good study Bible for your Scripture reading instead of a basic Bible. Rather than just praying alone, seek out a prayer partner or prayer group. If you love to journal, buy one that gets you interacting with and meditating on God's thoughts as they're communicated through His Word.

Biblically speaking, you can grow upward and grow downward in your love for Christ at the same time. As you do, you'll grow outward too. All three are godly pursuits. Just make sure you're growing.

Think About It: If you only throw seed on the surface of the soil, some shoots may sprout, but they won't stand for long. Going deep is the stabilizer for going up.

73

BULLETPROOF

Let's approach God with a sincere heart in full assurance of faith, having our hearts sprinkled clean from an evil conscience.

HEBREWS 10:22

The apostle Paul once advised a young cohort, "Cling to your faith in Christ, and keep your conscience clear" (1 Timothy 1:19 NLT). What good does that do? It's like putting on a bulletproof vest against the enemy's rounds of accusation.

Satan looks for every chance to condemn us, heaping lie upon lie, shame upon shame, and blame upon blame. Sometimes, to make matters even worse, he uses other people as his mouthpieces.

Think of Job's friends, who proposed that Job had brought his sufferings upon himself because God had deserted him for some unconfessed sin. (Meanwhile, *God* called their friend "a blameless and upright man" [Job 1:8]). In 2 Samuel 16, as David was fleeing Jerusalem to escape his son Absalom, a citizen named Shimei threw stones and kept cursing at Israel's king for his adultery with Bathsheba and for arranging the murder of her husband, Uriah.

Shimei wasn't entirely wrong. David *had* sinned greatly, and Absalom's uprising *was* one of those consequences. So we could understand if David thought, *Maybe God is still angry with me, like Shimei said.*

Yet David knew God, and he knew God's grace. And that made the difference.

You see, David had fully repented, so he was fully forgiven and fully restored in his relationship with God (Psalm 51). That's why he didn't lie awake second-guessing what Shimei had said. Instead, he put himself—both life and soul—in God's hands and slept soundly, sure of his salvation in the Lord (Psalm 3:5, 8).

What a picture of the power of God's grace! The Puritan preacher Thomas Watson once wrote that "a good conscience can sleep in the mouth of a cannon; grace is a Christian's coat of armor, which fears not the arrow or bullet. True grace may be shot at—but can never be shot through."

Armed with a clear conscience, the redeemed of the Lord can live in peace, rest in peace, and cry out to Him in peace, fully assured that they are safe in God.

Think About It: Satan will try to condemn you with lies, but a clear conscience will defend you in truth.

DEMOLISHING FORTRESSES

The weapons of our warfare are not of the flesh,
but divinely powerful for the destruction of fortresses.
We are destroying arguments and all arrogance raised
against the knowledge of God, and we are taking
every thought captive to the obedience of Christ.

2 CORINTHIANS 10:4-5

Though God can bring down any worldly fortress built against Him, He has also equipped His army to destroy the intellectual arguments, personal attitudes, or cultural ideas that oppose Him. Here are a few subtle yet divinely powerful "weapons" He provides for carrying out the mission:

Godly discernment. Whether worldly messages come wrapped like a "gift of enlightenment" or come at us like a hostile army storming the gates, we can prevent them from infiltrating our minds and hearts by knowing the Bible and "test[ing] the spirits to see whether they are from God" (1 John 4:1).

Humility. While it is a Christian's duty to "refuse foolish and ignorant speculations," we "must not be quarrelsome, but be kind to all...patient when wronged, with gentleness correcting those who are in opposition" (2 Timothy 2:23-25). God sometimes uses our humility and gracious responses to surprise people and bring them to their senses so they may "escape from the snare of the devil" (verse 26).

Self-control. The Holy Spirit empowers God's people to "abstain from fleshly lusts" and to keep our behavior "excellent" so that when unbelievers try to slander us, they find only good deeds instead and glorify God (1 Peter 2:11-12). Controlling our tongues and our emotions matters too (James 1:19), as does working to take captive any ideas or thoughts of our own that don't honor Christ.

Maybe you grew up immersed in lies, and some of those false beliefs are still roaming around in your mind and heart. Don't give them another day. Put on the armor of God, take up the sword of the Spirit—God's Word (Ephesians 6:10-18)—and with the help of fellow Christians (and maybe also a professional counselor), search out and destroy those ideas once and for all.

Think About It: Yes, you feel with your flesh, but you shouldn't fight with your flesh. Try your faith instead. Because then you will experience your Father fighting for you.

75

PRESS IN

The hour is coming, and is now here, when the true worshipers will worship the Father in spirit and truth, for the Father is seeking such people to worship him.

JOHN 4:23 ESV

It's not hard to put yourself in Sarah's and Abraham's sandals while they waited 25 excruciating years for Isaac to be conceived...

Month after month goes by—and not even a hint of morning sickness. Come year 10 or 12, and your faith has worn thin. *Did we hear correctly?*

Next thing you know, you're devising a work-around for the sake of some closure. *Maybe* this *is how God will fulfill His promise. Maybe my maidservant is supposed to birth our heir rather than me in my old age.* And you figure, *Why not? If this plan succeeds, the wait will be over!*

But wait! That's not the point.

If your wait is getting extra-long, this is the time to double down and press in to the Lord. Not only are you building endurance, which makes you "complete" (James 1:4), but Paul wrote that from the midst of suffering he was "reaching forward to what lies ahead" and "press[ing] on toward the goal for the prize of the upward call of God in Christ Jesus" (Philippians 3:13-14). Do you hear that? His suffering instilled more confidence in God's call on his life!

You may feel like backing off from God since He seems to have gone silent. You'll almost certainly want to devise an alternate plan, like Sarah did. But staying where God has you and continuing to worship Him in Spirit and in truth is the surest way through.

If you need extra wisdom or encouragement, speak up and ask for more. "Our generous God…will give it to you. He will not rebuke you for asking" (James 1:5 NLT). And while you're at it, you can be honest with Him about your weariness and disappointment. Many books of the Bible include laments, where the righteous pleaded, "How long, O Lord?" But skip the worldly solutions or the pursuit of your own ideas. "God [your] King is from of old, working salvation in the midst of the earth" (Psalm 74:12 ESV)—and in the midst of your suffering. Let God alone be your help and deliverance.

Think About It: In Psalm 69, the waters of adversity were up to David's neck, and he admitted his hope in the Lord was fading. But rather than giving up, he pressed in to the One who had proven steadfast and faithful already. Pray through this psalm if you're running low on hope right now.

MOVING UP

Let them do good, that they be rich in good works, ready to give, willing to share, storing up for themselves a good foundation for the time to come.

1 TIMOTHY 6:18-19 NKJV

As you wait for God to answer a long-awaited prayer or fulfill His call on your life, nothing is more demoralizing than a standstill. Except for maybe a setback. Setbacks and standstills are tough to navigate because they seem to keep us from God's will. God, however, always has a way forward, a way up. That's what He cares about. He wants to lift you up—making you ready for the next thing, preparing you for your promotion.

The next time you think you're standing still or you've been sent in reverse, aim for Joseph's approach. Young Joe had no idea how God's plan would pan out. All he understood was that one day he would rule over his brothers. But almost as soon as God delivered the dream, Joseph was being distanced from it—by others.

First, his brothers dumped him in a pit. Next, they sold him to slave traders, who sold him to an Egyptian official. Joe did everything right, but false charges landed him in prison. There, he earned everyone's trust, interpreted other prisoners' dreams; they promised to recommend him to Pharaoh—but then they didn't. Joe's reputation was stellar, but years later, he was still there in the cellar, until finally it was time for God to deliver him before Pharaoh.

From his teen years until probably his thirties, others kept setting Joseph back. In spite of these circumstances, he steadily progressed in the ways he could: proving faithful in all he was given to do, and like young Jesus, increasing "in wisdom and stature, and in favor with God and with people" (Luke 2:52 HCSB).

There's no telling what others will do that might distance you from the dream God has for you. Just don't separate *yourself* from it by choices that move you backward or sideways. Hold on to your integrity, do good, serve well, and cling to God. He can use the pit or the prison to prepare you for the palace. He can use opposition to open up opportunities. And, for sure, He can use your setbacks and standstills to strengthen you.

Christians, when God calls you, He's elevating you. Now it's time for you to move on up based on His Word.

Think About It: You can do everything right in a situation, and some people will still do you wrong. But whatever others do, you do the one thing you can do: Stay faithful to the Lord.

77

SPEAK LIFE

Let the words of my mouth and the meditation of my heart be acceptable in your sight, O Lord.

PSALM 19:14 ESV

In the previous two readings, we've seen negatively through Sarah and positively through Joseph the importance of how you conduct yourself while you wait on God to work His plan in your life. I would add to that: Be careful what you tell yourself.

If your wait ends up longer than you'd planned, after a while, you might find yourself saying what Israel was saying in Isaiah 40:27: "My way is hidden from the Lord." In other words, *He's forgotten me. He doesn't hear my prayers; He doesn't see my tears.* You might even begin to believe, *He's neglecting me. God is withholding from me.* In these times most of all—while you wait for God to move, or answer, or fulfill a promise—be careful what you say to yourself.

David was anointed Israel's future king while still in his teens, yet it was roughly 15 years before God's promise came to fruition. And those years included a lot of persecution at the hands of his predecessor, Saul, whom David faithfully served. Yet still David said:

- "You, Lord, are forgiving and good, abounding in love to all who call to you...When I am in distress, I call to you, because you answer me" (Psalm 86:5, 7 NIV).
- "I will watch for You, for God is my refuge. My God in His faithfulness will meet me; God will let me look triumphantly upon my enemies" (Psalm 59:9-10).
- "I will sing of Your strength; yes, I will joyfully sing of Your faithfulness in the morning, for You have been my refuge and a place of refuge on the day of my distress. My strength, I will sing praises to You; for God is my refuge, the God who shows me favor" (Psalm 59:16-17).

In a time of trouble, the sons of Korah, who were Levites and ancient worship leaders, sang this: "Why are you cast down, O my soul, and why are you in turmoil within me? Hope in God; for I shall again praise him, my salvation and my God" (Psalm 42:5-6 ESV).

Solomon wrote that "the words of a man's mouth are deep waters" and that "death and life are in the power of the tongue" (Proverbs 18:4, 21 ESV). Be careful to speak life and truth over yourself.

Think About It: Do your words match your faith or your feelings? The goal is for your feelings to catch up to your faith, not for your faith to succumb to your feelings. Your words can help you achieve that goal.

78

YOU HAD ME AT HELLO

As each one has received a special gift, employ it in serving one another as good stewards of the multifaceted grace of God. Whoever speaks is to do so as one who is speaking actual words of God; whoever serves is to do so as one who is serving by the strength which God supplies; so that in all things God may be glorified through Jesus Christ.

1 PETER 4:10-11

News flash: If you said hello and had a conversation with a stranger this weekend at church, that gift of welcoming someone naturally—not just when the pastor told you to shake hands and say hi—may have been the most important thing that happened to that person during their visit.

That's not me stating a "ministerial hypothetical." The folks at the *Baptist Bulletin* published a list titled "12 Turnoffs for Newcomers" about the things that deter first-time visitors from coming back to a church. Near the top of that list were "Grumpy Greeters" and "Unfriendly People." Simply by *not* being in one of those two categories, you could be a main reason that someone returns to your church next week.

It's not just about the preaching and the music, like some

people think. The genuine warmth of church members is like a glowing fire on a cold night. And the more those who are lost in darkness are exposed to the light—the light of the gospel, the Light of the world (Christ), the light emanating from all us sinners who have been saved by grace, and the light of Jesus in you personally—the less "draw" the darkness will have.

In the seats of every church on a given Sunday are single people, businesspeople, babies, families, divorced people, former drunks, widows, newlyweds, lost people, single moms, discouraged people, hungry people, high school students, and those who are being abused, mistreated, or ignored within their own families or social circles. They need somebody to care for them, connect with them, and share the love of Jesus with them.

Through you, "God makes a home for the lonely" (Psalm 68:6). Through you, the body of Christ dispels the darkness and operates like it's supposed to, with all hands and feet (and ears and elbows and knees) on deck, working as one, with Christ at the helm. Through you, someone this coming week may be introduced to the multifaceted grace of God for the very first time.

Think About It: Paul said, "I do all things for the sake of the gospel" (1 Corinthians 9:23). Do you?

TRAINED AND READY

It is for this we labor and strive,
because we have set our hope on the living God,
who is the Savior of all mankind, especially of believers.

1 TIMOTHY 4:10

Judging by the number of sports references he used in his writing, the apostle Paul must've been either athletic himself or a legitimate sports fan. He even urged the young pastor Timothy, "Train yourself to be godly. For physical training is of some value, but godliness has value for all things" (1 Timothy 4:7-8 NIV).

Besides cultivating "muscle-building" disciplines like prayer, Bible-reading, and Scripture memorization, be sure to push yourself in these ways:

Limit your exposure to worldly messages. You have to control who and what gets past the gates of your heart, mind, and eyes. Set digital locks and timers on your screens, be selective about who you follow on social media, and steer clear of office, neighborhood, or even church gossip. Also regularly assess yourself, asking: *Is anything I'm doing drawing me closer to the world rather than to Christ?* James 4:4 warns, "Whoever wants to be a friend of the world makes himself an enemy of God."

Be quick to cut out unhealthy or untrue thoughts. But don't stop there. Replace them with truths that are straight from Scripture.

Pursue accountability with fellow believers. Training as a team through Christian fellowship helps us gain strength and knowledge. And having truth spoken into our lives helps us "grow to become in every respect" part of "the mature body of him who is the head, that is, Christ" (Ephesians 4:15 NIV).

Keep a clean slate with the Lord through repentance and confession. When you know you are right with Him, you won't shrink back in shame or fear when Satan comes at you. You'll stand your ground, confident that "there is now no condemnation *at all* for those who are in Christ Jesus" (Romans 8:1).

One of the best things about spiritual training is that it holds promise "for the present life and also for the life to come" (1 Timothy 4:8). A two-for-one, now-and-forever deal. It doesn't get any better than that!

Think About It: The spirit and flesh are in a boxing match inside the ring of your soul. Whichever one of those fighters you feed will win. The one you starve will lose.

80

OVER IT

The Lord is compassionate and gracious,
slow to anger and abounding in mercy…
He has not dealt with us according to our sins,
nor rewarded us according to our guilty deeds.

PSALM 103:8, 10

Some of the Christians I've met over the years are living bound up in the fear that they can never be forgiven for some sin of the past, even though they've repented again and again. In their minds, what they've done is just too big to ever be wiped clean. I feel for them, because while that sin is long gone in God's eyes, they are still carrying around a supersized burden of guilt.

Christ, however, handled all of it. He did the heavy lifting of sin, and He did it so we wouldn't be crushed by the guilt of sin either.

The following verses tell us about the *extent* of God's forgiveness: "As high as the heavens are above the earth, so great is His mercy toward those who fear Him. As far as the east is from the west, so far has He removed our wrongdoings from us" (Psalm 103:11-12). His forgiveness has no limits. It isn't like some of the coupons my wife uses when she goes to the store: good for the smaller-sized item, but don't try applying it toward the bulk size. No sin is too bulky for the coupon of God's grace! Regardless of what you've done, you cannot out-sin His ability to forgive and forget. His mercy reaches "as high as the heavens are above the earth."

That's hard to fathom, I know. For a little perspective, Neptune is the farthest planet from the earth in our solar system—well over 2.5 billion miles into the stratosphere—and still the heavens keep going. Wherever God has established the physical borders of space, the eternal heaven begins. So never fear. As soon as you confessed your supersized sin and turned away from it, that was it. Gone. Done deal. Erased from heaven's memory, never to be recalled again.

If the holy God whom you sinned against most of all has put it behind Him, you can do the same. It's time to stop punishing yourself. Time to quit recounting to Him or yourself what you did back then. He's over it. Now you can be too.

Think About It: If the judge has declared you not guilty, then you are free to *not* walk in guilt. God has not only declared it, but by His grace, He has made it so. You are free!

WISDOM FOR BREAKFAST

Know also that wisdom is like honey for you:
If you find it, there is a future hope for you,
and your hope will not be cut off.

PROVERBS 24:14 NIV

For generations, Wheaties cereal has been known as "The Breakfast of Champions." Their cereal boxes have highlighted more than 850 athletes and teams from various eras, starting with baseball great Lou Gehrig in 1934 and featuring Olympic gold-medal gymnast Simone Biles twice in 2022. Making it onto a box of Wheaties means you've made it big in the world of sports. But did you ever wonder how many of those champions actually ate Wheaties for breakfast? My guess is *almost none*.

I'll tell you what *will* make you a champion: wisdom for breakfast. God's Word is that vital, that nutrient-rich—"beneficial for teaching, for rebuke, for correction, for training in righteousness; so that the man or woman of God may be fully capable, equipped for every good work" (2 Timothy 3:16-17). Plus, it's not something we have to force down our throats: "How sweet are Your words to my taste! Yes, sweeter than honey to my mouth! From your precepts I get understanding" (Psalm 119:103-4).

The prophet Isaiah remarked: "The Sovereign LORD has given me a well-instructed tongue, to know the word that sustains the weary. He wakens me morning by morning, wakens my ear to listen like one being instructed" (Isaiah 50:4 NIV). Paul encouraged Timothy, who had been raised by a Christian mother and grandmother, to "continue in what you have learned...from childhood," which is that "the sacred Scriptures...are able to give you wisdom for salvation through faith in Christ Jesus" (2 Timothy 3:14-15 HCSB).

Don't just consume wisdom for breakfast either. It's for lunch and dinner too. The very first words of the book of Psalms include a blessing on the person whose "delight is in the law of the LORD, and on his law he meditates *day and night*" (1:2 ESV). God's Word will strengthen you for the battles of your day and keep you strong like nothing else. Get yourself a full serving before you walk out the door.

Think About It: People always ask: "Why can't sweet things be good for you?" Well, here's your chance to take in something sweet that will make you healthier than you've ever been.

RESISTANCE EFFORTS

Walk by the Spirit, and you will not carry out the desire of the flesh. For the desire of the flesh is against the Spirit, and the Spirit against the flesh; for these are in opposition to one another.

GALATIANS 5:16-17

We see one of Satan's favorite battle maneuvers in his conversation with Eve in Genesis 3. The serpent questioned, "Did God actually say, 'You shall not eat of any tree in the garden'?" while fully knowing the answer. Once Eve specified that one tree was off-limits, the serpent countered, "You will not surely die" (verses 1, 4 ESV).

What was Satan doing? He was baiting her toward temptation by saying, "C'mon, it's okay; do what you want," just like he does with each of us. There's a reason our enemy uses this tactic: because he knows how much our flesh—the ego and selfish drive of our sin nature—loves a yes. "When the woman saw that the tree was good for food, and that it was a delight to the eyes, and that the tree was to be desired to make one wise, she took of its fruit and ate, and she also gave some to her husband who was with her, and he ate" (Genesis 3:6 ESV).

You can just see the wheels turning in Eve's head. *The fruit is pretty and looks tasty...and it can make me wise. Check, check, and check. Sounds like a yes to me!* But the Lord had already given Adam and Eve a hard no about eating from that tree. In this instance, His word should've been their one and only directive.

In addition to His Word, God has sent us further reinforcements in the resistance effort. Not only do we have the camaraderie of other Christian soldiers, but every person who has said yes to Jesus's rule and reign in their life has His Spirit, the Holy Spirit, literally empowering them "to abstain from the passions of the flesh, which wage war against your soul" (1 Peter 2:11 ESV).

Pastor John Piper has said, "The sign of whether you are indwelt by the Spirit is not that you have no bad desires, but that you are at war with them!...The winner of that war will be the Spirit."[11]

The winner will be the Spirit—assuming you invite Him into every decision, every temptation, every consideration. Don't hesitate to call on Him.

Think About It: If you have the inner battle, that's evidence you are saved for heaven. If you are led by the Spirit in the battle, now you are also saved on earth. Walk in your salvation.

83

LOOK WHO'S TALKING

You light my lamp; the LORD
my God illumines my darkness.

PSALM 18:28

Though God clearly stated His desire regarding the fruit of the one tree in Eden, discerning His voice from all other voices is not always easy for us. Is our flesh being manipulated by the enemy, giving us the yes we think we want to hear? Or is the Spirit of God giving us the green light from above?

The Word of God is our compass for discernment. But there are plenty of times in life when the compass isn't clearly pointing in a direction—maybe it's a gray area biblically, or you're not seeing where Scripture speaks to your situation at all. Don't despair. The Holy Spirit illumines our minds to God's will and the deciphering of God's Word anytime we ask. So before you do anything else, take your questions to Him. Then follow up with this checklist of questions to ask yourself:

Does this yes go against God's Word in any way? Is there anything unfruitful about it? Go down the list: "The fruit of the Spirit is love, joy, peace, patience, kindness, goodness, faithfulness, gentleness, self-control" (Galatians 5:22-23). "The wisdom from above," wrote James, "is first pure, then peace-loving, gentle, reasonable, full of mercy and good fruits, impartial, free of hypocrisy. And the fruit of righteousness is sown in peace by those who make peace" (James 3:17-18).

Is it life-giving? Will it protect you and those you are responsible for? Proverbs 11:30 reminds us, "The fruit of the righteous is a tree of life, and the one who is wise saves lives" (NIV). The psalmist prayed, "Incline my heart to your testimonies, and not to selfish gain! Turn my eyes from looking at worthless things; and give me life in your ways" (Psalm 119:36-37 ESV).

Will this draw me closer to Christ? Anything that would put even a speck of distance between you and Him is not the Holy Spirit talking.

If, after this, you're still not sure whether this yes can be trusted, seek out some wise Christian counsel…then wait. Given time, the Holy Spirit will bring you to certainty or strong peace in one direction. At that point, no more delay. Obey. It's go time!

Think About It: You're waiting on God's will, not the yes of the flesh. The life of the Spirit, not the enticement of the eyes. Going the right way is better than going right now.

84

ALIENS AMONG US

By faith [Abraham] lived as an alien in the land of promise...for he was looking for the city which has foundations, whose architect and builder is God.

HEBREWS 11:9-10 NASB1995

It's a topic of lively discussion lately. Social media, the internet, Congress—everybody seems to be inquiring: *Do aliens exist?* I can end the debate right here and now. Yes, aliens exist on planet earth; they're also known as Christians.

Need proof? Scripture refers to the Israelites as "aliens" while they were in Egypt (Deuteronomy 10:19 NASB1995; Acts 7:6 NASB1995). Before Israel occupied the promised land, the Lord declared, "You are but aliens and sojourners with Me" (Leviticus 25:23 NASB1995). And Peter wrote "to those who reside as aliens, scattered throughout Pontus, Galatia, Cappadocia, Asia, and Bithynia" (1 Peter 1:1 NASB1995).

Hebrews 11 additionally describes the faithful saints from the annals of Scripture as those who "confessed that they were strangers and exiles on the earth" (verse 13). The writer also observes, "Those who say such things make it clear that they are seeking a country of their own," not a place they've already been (verse 14). They're forward-moving, forward-thinking people who "desire a better country, that is, a heavenly one," prepared by God just for them (verse 16).

Now obviously, Scripture's version of "aliens" isn't little green creatures from another planet. We *are*, however, a supernatural race and citizens of another realm. Only we are not born into this physically. We are "chosen," wrote Peter, "according to the foreknowledge of God the Father, by the sanctifying work of the Spirit, to obey Jesus Christ and be sprinkled with His blood" (1 Peter 1:1-2). We've been spiritually "born again to a living hope through the resurrection of Jesus Christ from the dead" (verse 3). As a result, we receive an inheritance reserved for us in heaven (verses 3-4).

So anytime you're feeling like someone who doesn't fit in—who looks and acts and thinks different than the people around you—realize this: You're not wrong. You and I are only visiting this planet. Our current address is not our permanent address. Our mail is even now being forwarded to the city of God. And that hope and longing for heaven inside of you? It's been put there to stay. Your Maker is using it to guide you home.

Think About It: Your longing for a better place is evidence that a better place exists. Until you get there, your job is to make this place look more like home.

85

TOGETHER

We urge you, brothers and sisters, admonish the unruly, encourage the fainthearted, help the weak, be patient with everyone...Always seek what is good for one another and for all people.

1 THESSALONIANS 5:14-15

Many battles of life and faith are won by the hope and help of our brothers and sisters in the Lord. Remember these from Scripture?

- Aaron and Hur holding up Moses's arms to secure victory for the army of Israel (Exodus 17:8-13).
- Saul's son Jonathan protecting David from his father and further risking his life to encourage his friend in the Lord (1 Samuel 19–20).
- The servants of the leprous army commander Naaman urging him to maintain humility in his desire for healing (2 Kings 5:1-14).
- The men tearing through a roof to bring their friend to Jesus for healing (Luke 5:17-20, 24-25).

- Ananias and Barnabas advocating for the new convert, Paul, so his preaching of the gospel would not be hindered by the skepticism of the brethren (Acts 9:10-27).
- The local church praying fervently and holding prayer vigils for Peter's release from prison (Acts 12:1-17).

Friends, this is how we do it in God's family. This is the body of Christ in action—each person building up, challenging, and spurring others to greater faith in God.

Whose arms can you hold up today? Who in your life needs a boost of faith, some vigilant prayer, or a word of refreshing? Don't wait for someone else to do it. *You* do it. Be the one who steps forward and says, "I'll help. I'll stand by your side." And don't forget the Christians you look up to—pastors, mentors, teachers, the prayer warriors you know. They may seem like spiritual giants who need nothing, but trust me, as a pastor myself and a pastor's kid, your encouragement and prayers help keep us going in the midst of *our* battles.

We're all in this together. *Together.* That's how victories are won.

Think About It: Strength for your battle comes when you are there for someone else. When your focus is on another, you are restored too (Job 42:10).

86

THE CHAMPION

The LORD *is with me like a powerful champion;*
therefore my persecutors will stumble and not prevail.

JEREMIAH 20:11

In Jeremiah 20, we read that Pashhur, a priest and the overseer of the house of the Lord, persecuted Jeremiah for his prophetic words. But it wasn't only Pashhur who was oppressing God's servant. Jeremiah had become "a laughingstock all day long" (verse 7). "Everyone mocks me," he said; "for me the word of the LORD has resulted in taunting and derision" (verses 7-8). Even Jeremiah's friends were watching for him to falter in his testimony (verse 10). *Maybe he'll give it up,* they thought. *If we denounce him, maybe he will shut up.*

Can you relate? Your coworkers, your family, or your friends are shunning you, making fun of you, hoping you'll "just stop with the Jesus stuff." It's possible your loyalty to the Lord is even embarrassing enough to some passionless Christians that they're distancing themselves from you. But in the midst of his laments to God, Jeremiah laid claim to a truth that would sustain him in completing his godly mission and purpose: "The LORD is with me like a powerful champion" (verse 11).

I don't know about you, but I regularly need this reminder of who God is so I can continue in the fight. Because the truth is, when you're on the frontlines, the last person you want beside you is somebody who's lukewarm or weak-minded or quick to quit. You need someone who understands what you're up against and knows how to win. A veteran of war who is fearless and strong and will have your back. Not someone who will abandon you or turn against you at the first hint of opposition.

If Jeremiah and countless other soldiers of the faith over the centuries were brave enough to do battle based on this one assurance, so can you and I. As you take up your battle position today, be bold. The Champion of heaven and earth is with you.

Think About It: Sometimes you must choose between human validation and God's validation. While human validation may feel good, God's validation *is* good. Choose wisely.

SUITED UP

This is why you must take up the full armor of God,
so that you may be able to resist in the evil day,
and having prepared everything, to take your stand.

EPHESIANS 6:13 HCSB

I know I've talked a lot in this book about how Satan operates. That's not to scare you but to equip you.

Our adversary isn't only an opportunist who seizes on our moments of weakness. He is also a planner, a strategist. He has *schemes* (Ephesians 6:11), just like our opponents always did in football. Each week, they prepared a specific game plan with us in mind—one they thought would deny us the victory and give them a win.

The devil, in coordination with his personnel, does the same with you and me. He scouts us. He watches our game film to learn our individual strengths and weaknesses. He pays attention to our tendencies, notes our patterns, and then uses all that "intel" to plot against us. And he would like nothing better than for every Christian to face-plant in the dirt.

It doesn't matter to him whether it's the dirt of sin such as bitterness, selfishness, lust, arrogance, workaholism, deceit, or hatred—or whether you're buried by adversity such as illness, rejection, grief, or financial struggles. He will use anything, try anything, to break down your defenses and run you over.

That's why you have to suit up, like Ephesians 6:13-17 describes. A football player who takes the field without his helmet, pads, and cleats is going to get pummeled. But putting on the armor of truth, righteousness, peace, faith, and sure salvation each day is your ironclad protection. And with the sword of the Spirit (the Word of God) in hand, you are truly formidable.

Ephesians 6 communicates how important a constant attitude of prayer is too. Satan doesn't spend much time scheming against the "Hail Mary" pray-ers who only call on God when they need a last-minute miracle. He doesn't have to. It's the Christians who "pray at all times in the Spirit" for themselves and other believers who present his biggest challenge (verse 18).

Armor. Sword. Prayer. Once you've readied yourself with the equipment Christ has provided, there's no way the enemy can defeat you.

Think About It: You have to suit up, keep your sword up, and stay prayed up to be able to stand up to the enemy's schemes.

ALL-SEASON FAITH

Love the LORD your God with all your heart,
with all your soul, and with all your strength.
These words that I am giving you today are to be in your heart.

DEUTERONOMY 6:5-6 HCSB

We get some insight into how Satan operates in Job 1 and 2. We especially get a glimpse of his long game, when he can't easily trap his target.

In both chapters, the devil admits to God that he's been "roaming" the earth. He's been out there hunting for his next victim. God cites Job as a shining example of someone who hasn't fallen prey to Satan's schemes. At hearing this, the adversary grows agitated. He's probably had his eye on Job for a long time, but he hasn't been able to bring down God's man.

Satan protests that it's because God is safeguarding him: "Have you not put a hedge around him and his household and everything he has?...Now stretch out your hand and strike everything he has, and he will surely curse you to your face" (1:10-11 NIV).

When that idea fails to have the intended effect, Satan switches to another plan of attack, convinced that Job can be defeated if

God will let him mess with Job's health (2:5). But again, Job does not turn his back on God or blame God for what has happened.

That was something the devil wasn't counting on. Knowing human nature as he does, he figured Job was like so many other religious types: someone who is all about prospering from God but not persevering in God. But Job didn't just love and obey the Lord for His gifts. He didn't just remain faithful as long as life was good. He was fully committed—heart, soul, mind, and strength.

Every one of us should strive to be a Job in our time. One who frustrates and foils the devil and who God can boast in.

Surface spirituality won't cut it. You can't hang out among the fair-weather faithful. You have to be an all-season Christian. Job was the same person in triumph and tragedy, a man who, as God described, still held to his integrity after disaster struck (2:3). Job had lots of questions for God. His grief was gut-wrenching. Yet his faith remained intact. May the same be true of you and me.

Think About It: Is Satan frustrated by your faith and commitment when he challenges you? It's frustrating for any defense when they hit their hardest and the offense still scores. "Resist the devil, and he will flee from you" (James 4:7 ESV).

89

NO CASUALTIES

We are not ignorant of [Satan's] schemes.

2 CORINTHIANS 2:11

Dr. David Jeremiah has said that in the very real spiritual battle in which we are involved, "those least in the know are often the first casualties."[12] No Christian, though, ever has to be a casualty of this war.

To take a page from my football-playing days: Don't hesitate to scout out who you're up against. Get to know your adversary's strengths, weaknesses, and tendencies, like he does with you. Then ask the Holy Spirit to help you develop a strategy following the divine Playbook you've been given—all to throw Satan off his game.

Where can you learn more about the enemy? Start with Scripture. The Bible contains the authoritative history on him, revealing his background, his motives, and his methods. It has the downlow on Satan's maneuvers; who is most susceptible to his tactics; how he blinds, fools, and exploits people; and which actions shut down his efforts. Some additional "scouting reports" worth reading are *The Screwtape Letters* by C.S. Lewis, *Fighting Satan* by Joel R. Beeke, and *The Strategy of Satan* by Warren W. Weirsbe.

The truth is, due to his limited powers and inability to come up with new ideas, the devil's playbook isn't all that big. On the other hand, our Creator God is infinite. He has limitless ways to confuse and frustrate what Satan is doing, and God will coach you in foiling any plan set against you.

This scouting and strategizing will help you follow God's game plan as situations unfold. The Holy Spirit is the One who sends in the play calls from above (John 16:13; 1 Corinthians 2:10). Sometimes, depending on what the enemy is doing, you'll be asked to make adjustments on the field. Don't argue. Trust what He tells you and where He positions you. The quicker you adjust, the sooner you score.

Think About It: Since the devil has schemes, we must have a strategy to advance against his schemes. If he has schemes and we have no strategy, then we don't stand a chance.

ON OFFENSE

I am sending you out as sheep in the midst of wolves, so be wise as serpents and innocent as doves.

MATTHEW 10:16 ESV

Once you're trained in defending against Satan's tactics, you can go back to playing offense, focusing on God and His purposes for you.

As I picture it, the best way to excel at playing offense biblically is to get yourself in peak spiritual condition and then keep yourself in peak condition. And based on Jesus's words in Matthew 10:16, two main areas of concentration should be wisdom and innocence. You increase *wisdom* by devoting yourself to God and His truth, and deepening your relationship with Christ. Knowledge without relationship only takes you so far in your faith. But when you know Christ *and* His Word intimately, you're strengthening both your heart and your mind.

Keep developing your sword skills too. Study the Bible every day so you're learning to wield it effectively. Unlike man-made swords, your spiritual sword gets sharper the more you use it. You become quicker to recognize subtle schemes. Quicker to block sin before it becomes a stronghold. Quicker to offer grace and mercy. And tougher in general for the enemy to bring down.

A way to increase *innocence* is to do things that prevent sin in the first place and keep you "from being polluted by the world" (James 1:27 NIV). Like avoiding exposure to temptation or tempting environments. It's also a good idea to ask the Holy Spirit to help you devise specific-to-you strategies that can strengthen you. As an example, since Scripture teaches that Satan seeks to sabotage every believer's thinking, consider: When does he tend to undermine *you* with worry or anxiety? What are the ways he has tried to limit your beliefs about who Jesus is or what God can do? How does he typically distract you in your time with God? He's going to aim first where he's had the most success in the past. You know this, so anticipate it.

Shore up those weak spots. Ask other Christians what they do to set their minds on things above (Colossians 3:2) and adhere to their spiritual disciplines. And get counseling for any past wounds that are affecting your thinking. God has every insight and idea you'll ever need, and He is committed to making you wiser and more innocent in all your ways.

Think About It: You can't expect to play well against your opponent if you don't practice. Practice doesn't make perfect, but it does make you proficient when dealing with an adversary.

91

GOD IN THE EQUATION

Blessed are those who keep his testimonies,
who seek him with their whole heart,
who also do no wrong, but walk in his ways!

PSALM 119:2-3 ESV

Thinking they knew best, the people of Scripture took matters into their own hands, and in each case, we know how *that* turned out...

- Adam and Eve ate what looked like the finest fruit in the garden, and they reaped a world of hurt (Genesis 3).
- Moses struck the rock to produce water rather than speaking to it as the Lord had specified, and he was denied entrance into the promised land (Numbers 20:2-13).
- The people of Israel demanded a human king, "that we also may be like all the nations, and that our king may...go out before us and fight our battles" (1 Samuel 8:20 ESV). Yet the appointed one, Saul, not only failed to keep his throne but also failed to go to battle for those very same people (1 Samuel 17:11).

- Jonah opted to flee the Lord's presence rather than evangelize the enemy, and he landed himself in a situation he couldn't stomach (Jonah 1–2).
- Ananias and his wife, Sapphira, lied about keeping some of the proceeds from a piece of land they sold, and they paid with their lives (Acts 5:1-11).

As for you, when was the last time you left God out of the equation, thinking you had a better answer? Most likely, you chose what looked good in the moment. Or what promised instant results. Or what made *you* more comfortable.

We've all done it—and we've all arrived at the same result: Our human solutions, minus God, ultimately equate to zero. Thankfully, none of us has to be an Einstein to figure out the answer to our problem, whatever our problem may be. It's a two-part process: First, start with God as the X factor in your situation, seeking Him with your whole heart. Then, obediently wait on Him for the answer. He's the only solution that makes everything else make sense.

Think About It: Our problem is not the real problem. Our disobedience to God within the problem we face is what's most problematic.

92

WAKE UP!

I know your deeds; you have a reputation of being alive, but you are dead. Wake up! Strengthen what remains and is about to die, for I have found your deeds unfinished in the sight of my God.

REVELATION 3:1-2 NIV

If you're intent on keeping your spiritual guard up, the ancient city of Sardis is a lesson in what not to do.

What's *that* story? In its glory days, Sardis had the reputation of being an impenetrable city because of where it was built. Sardis stood 1,500 feet above a remote valley and was bordered by a mountain and sheer cliffs that were almost impossible to climb. There was simply no way a big army could reach its heights and overthrow it.

Nevertheless, Sardis was captured twice. Were fiery arrows shot through the skies by hundreds of soldiers below? No. The "impenetrable city" was captured by a strategic commander with a small contingent of men who were as agile and quiet as ninjas.

Both times, Sardis's enemies were able to infiltrate and ransack the city by stealth in the middle of the night. How? That's the crazy part. Once they got up the cliffs, they simply entered through the city gates.

It was easy because the Sardians weren't keeping watch. They believed they were so safe inside their walls, they left the city gates unguarded while they slept.

Now Jesus's letter to the church at Sardis in Revelation 3 makes sense. Unless the believers there got serious again about things like upholding doctrine and being lights in the idol-worshiping darkness of their culture, that church was as good as dead. Their reputation wouldn't save them.

As a Christian, if you don't keep watch, you're vulnerable no matter how strong you are or how rock-solid your reputation has been. It simply doesn't take much to defeat someone who's sleeping on the job, sure that they're covered and have nothing to worry about. (Just ask Samson, whose story is found in Judges 16.)

This must be a reason why Paul urged the young pastor Timothy to not only "watch your life and doctrine closely" but to "persevere in them" (1 Timothy 4:16 NIV); and why Proverbs 4:23 reminds us, "Above all else, guard your heart, for everything you do flows from it" (NIV).

Think About It: In the spiritual war, overconfidence can be your downfall. Don't take anything for granted. Stay alert and keep watch every single day.

93

TIMING IS EVERYTHING

It is God who is at work in you,
both to desire and to work for His good pleasure.

PHILIPPIANS 2:13

In life, timing is everything.

Each one of my kids has asked for a snack just before dinner. Each of the older ones has wanted to put off their homework to play longer. Do my wife and I just acquiesce? No. Our children are still learning what's good for them—and when. In the meantime, we are teaching them to treat "wait" and "no" as valid answers.

Now apply that to your relationship with your Father in heaven. One of the most important things any child of God can understand is that a no from the Lord is a loving protection, not a punishment. He's not withholding from you to be cruel.

God's no doesn't necessarily mean "never" either (although, like the Israelites in the wilderness, we often grumble about it as if it does). Many times, it means: "Yes, but not yet." And when it's an outright no, it means: "I have something better in mind." Ever seen that in your own life? When you look back, you can see how God was preparing you, sparing you, by keeping you on His schedule?

We want our kids to patiently trust our timing, but how well are we modeling that as God's own sons and daughters? King Solomon observed, "There is an appointed time for everything. And there is a time for every matter under heaven" (Ecclesiastes 3:1). What is a no one day may be a yes some other day—all because *now* is suddenly the right time, when last time, for reasons known to God, it was the wrong time.

In one of his letters, the famous novelist Lewis Carroll wrote, "I have had prayers answered—most strangely so sometimes—but I think our heavenly Father's loving-kindness has been even more evident in what He has *refused* me."[13]

If the timing is all wrong, even the best things in life can set us back or be harmful. God's best awaits those who are willing to take the no to get to whatever His yes may be, *whenever* that may be.

Think About It: If your life is for His pleasure over and above your pleasure, then it's easier to submit to both His answer and His schedule. It's all about Him.

ASKED AND ANSWERED

All the promises of God find their "Yes" in him.

2 CORINTHIANS 1:20 ESV

We call them unanswered prayers, but God never lets any prayer of the righteous go unanswered. We just might not be getting the answers we were looking for.

I know that when my mom died, I really questioned whether God had heard. Or maybe He heard and just ignored us. With an unveiled face, I went to Him, demanding some answers. *Why didn't You do what we were praying for? Didn't You see the people who were circling my mom and dad's house, asking You to knock down the walls of this cancer like it was the city of Jericho? Didn't You hear the prayers of so many of Your people around the world?*

Your Word says that if we pray believing, we will receive. Your Word says we have victory in Jesus's name. Your Word commands us to be anxious for nothing, but through prayer and supplication, to make our requests known. We did all that. We asked that You would be glorified. But Mom's healing never came.

I was coming at God, and He came back at me. Through the conviction of His Spirit and through His Word, He let me know: "Jonathan, you're coming at Me wrong. First of all, you need to understand that I am sovereign, and My game plan is bigger than any one player on My field. So you need to trust in Me with all your heart, and do not lean on yourself but on Me. My ways are above your ways, and My thoughts are above your thoughts.

"Second of all, you're a preacher. You tell people all the time about My victory, and you don't even understand My victory. Just because I didn't answer your prayer *your* way doesn't mean I haven't already answered your prayer *anyway*. Because of the victory I have given you and your mom, there were always only two answers to your prayers: yes and yes. Either she was going to be healed…or she was going to be *healed*. Either she was going to live…or she was going to *live*. Either she was going to be with family…or she was going to be *with family*. My grace is sufficient for you."

In other words: Asked. And answered.

Think About It: Our circumstances can make us easily forget what will always be true: Neither life nor death can separate us from the love of God or the grace of God (Romans 8:38-39).

95

NO FEAR

[The one who trusts in the Lord] is like a tree planted by water, that sends out its roots by the stream, and does not fear when heat comes, for its leaves remain green, and is not anxious in the year of drought, for it does not cease to bear fruit.

JEREMIAH 17:8 ESV

A few years ago, *Psychology Today* highlighted a Penn State University study that found only about 10 percent of what we worry about actually ever comes to pass.[14] Other worry research backs this up. Yet I realize that favorable numbers rarely stop people from worrying.

The words of God don't automatically calm our fears either—at least not until we've absorbed them as unshakable truth. That's why I challenge you to keep coming back to strong verses and letting them sink in. Because they speak to far more than worry. They are God's comfort about the things we dread and the darknesses we fear most, such as death, suffering, or evil.

Psalm 23:4 says, "Even though I walk through the valley of the shadow of death, I fear no evil, for You are with me."

Proverbs 1:33 affirms, "Whoever listens to [wisdom] will live securely and will be at ease from the dread of evil."

Jesus says in John 11:25-26, "I am the resurrection and the life; the one who believes in Me will live, even if he dies, and everyone who lives and believes in Me will never die."

Romans 8:38 promises, "Neither death nor life…neither our fears for today nor our worries about tomorrow—not even the powers of hell can separate us from God's love" (NLT).

If you could use even more assurance to temper your fears, memorize this passage from Psalm 103:

> As a father has compassion on his children, so the LORD has compassion on those who fear [revere] Him. For He knows what we are made of, remembering that we are dust…From eternity to eternity the LORD's faithful love is toward those who fear Him…who remember to observe His precepts (verses 13-14, 17-18 HCSB).

And don't forget the comforting words of the Lord in Isaiah 41:10: "Do not fear, for I am with you; do not be afraid, for I am your God. I will strengthen you; I will help you; I will hold on to you with My righteous right hand" (HCSB).

Think About It: Do you believe He understands and He's with you? The Word says He is (Hebrews 4:15), so trust it.

96

AVOIDING HEART DISEASE

Just as we have been approved by God to be entrusted with the gospel, so we speak…to please God, who examines our hearts.

1 THESSALONIANS 2:4

Not only did Americans increase their binge-watching during the COVID-19 pandemic, but the *number* of Americans who binge-watched doubled, according to researcher Susan Carnell, PhD.[15] Even now, well past 2020, more Americans are binge-watching as a regular habit than before. It seems to be one of the lasting effects of the pandemic. In that sense, you could say that some people are acting like they're still locked down, even though they're no longer locked down!

Does that describe your Christian life or witness at all? For whatever reason, have you insulated inside your four walls, away from the world, where you're impacting almost no one? Have you distanced yourself from your church, uninterested in being involved? Are you more concerned with the comforts of your own little kingdom than you are with reaching the lost, helping others in need, or increasing your faith? For decades, medical science has been telling us that a passive lifestyle puts people on a fast track to disease and even death. For centuries, God's Word has been communicating the same thing spiritually.

Complacency in our faith not only makes us flabby, but it can also turn into spiritual heart disease. Here is how you know you're suffering from late-stage complacency:

- Your heartbeat for God and His Word is barely discernible.
- Your temperature toward outsiders is growing colder as you get more involved in your own interests.
- Your energy for reaching others with the gospel is rapidly decreasing.
- You're consuming liquids: spiritual milk and a watered-down message. No meat.

Whether you end up in this condition is entirely up to you. Thankfully, Christ's resurrection makes it entirely reversible as long as you're breathing. Don't wait another day, believer. Do whatever it takes to get up and get moving.

Think About It: A healthy lifestyle is a healthy life. An unhealthy lifestyle is an unhealthy life. Do you want to be spiritually healthy? Make it a lifestyle.

97

FOLLOW THE SON

I wait for the Lord, my whole being waits, and in his word I put my hope. I wait for the Lord more than watchmen wait for the morning.

PSALM 130:5-6 NIV

While all plants need sunlight, sunflowers are so utterly dependent on the sun that they follow its path across the sky, turning their faces a full 180 degrees from east to west each day. Then at night, they turn their heads back to the east in anticipation of the dawn.

Scientists have tracked this on video, and you can see the plants actually reorienting themselves after the sun sets.

Sunflowers watch for the sun. They wait for the sun to show up. And they position themselves so they're ready when it does appear.

You may be surrounded by the darkness of difficulty right now. The night may be falling heavy upon you, to the degree that you're feeling lost. But let me ask: Are you positioned to see the first hints of dawn on the horizon?

The difference for us as Christians is that we know—are guaranteed—that a new day is coming. "Weeping may endure for a night," wrote the psalmist, "but joy comes in the morning" (Psalm 30:5 NKJV). Someday, God will wipe every tear from the eyes of His people, "and death shall be no more, neither shall there be mourning, nor crying, nor pain anymore" (Revelation 21:4 ESV). Not only that, but there will be no more night whatsoever (Revelation 22:5). Jesus, the Son of God, will appear in the skies, shining forth "with power and great glory" (Luke 21:27). Then there will be no need for "the light of a lamp or the light of the sun" (Revelation 22:5 NIV), for the Lord God will be their Sun.

We can anticipate it because God promises it. We can look up and lift up our heads, not just because the peace of Christ and the comfort of the Holy Spirit are ours now, in the dark of night (John 14:26-27), but because our "redemption is drawing near" (Luke 21:28). Until then, like those sunflowers, let's wait in hope, "without wavering, for He who promised is faithful" (Hebrews 10:23).

Think About It: Let the shadows be evidence to you that there is light somewhere. We're prone to get lost in the shadows, but find the Light. Look for the Light and follow it.

98

FILM DAY

It is better to go to a house of mourning than to go to a house of feasting, because [death] is the end of every person, and the living takes it to heart.

ECCLESIASTES 7:2

One of my NFL coaches would always say, "Remember what's coming." Because we players knew what he meant, many of us would take the field on Sunday thinking about Monday. You know why? Because Monday was accountability day—the review of the game-day film.

On Monday, Coach would walk in, pull down the video screen, turn on the overhead projector, pick up his red pointer, and say, "All I want to know is: Did you do what we asked and play by our book, or were you were out there doing your own thing? Don't answer…We're about to watch it right now."

One day, the game of this life will be over for each of us, and God the Father will walk up, pull down His cosmic screen, turn on His Holy Ghost overhead projector, pick up His blood-of-Jesus red pointer, and ask: "Did you honor the logo that was on your helmet based on the Playbook I gave you? Did you sacrifice yourself out there on the field for the sake of the team like My Son did? Or were you out there doing your own thing? Don't answer that…We're about to watch it right now."

This is why Ecclesiastes 7 says it's better to go to a funeral than a party. Because the funeral reminds you who you're playing for, why you're playing, and how—*ahead of* Monday.

Jesus lived, died, and forever lives so you and I could bask eternally in celebration of victory. If you don't like how your film is shaping up, if you know your Coach won't be pleased, then go back to the Playbook. And while you're at it, do everything you can to study and pattern yourself after the team's forever Captain, Jesus, so that, come Monday, you'll hear the coveted words: "Well done…Come and share [My] happiness!" (Matthew 25:21 NIV).

Think About It: Keep tomorrow in mind as you live today, so that when tomorrow comes, you will have much to celebrate.

99

FINISH IT

The eyes of the LORD roam throughout the earth, so that He may strongly support those whose heart is completely His.

2 CHRONICLES 16:9

For 35 years, King Asa of Judah went faithfully to the Lord for direction, counsel, help, and protection. This was how he operated in times of peace and times of war. But for some reason, he backtracked in his later years. (You can find his story in 2 Chronicles 14–16.)

The first incident was when he asked another king to come to Judah's aid against the king of Israel. He resorted to human help rather than God's help, despite everything the Lord had done for him every time Asa sought Him out. Afterward, God sent a messenger to admonish Asa about the error of his ways and call him back to the ways of God. Instead, the king got angry, punishing Hanani, the seer. Not only that, but it looks like Asa may have remained angry at God because, three years later, when he developed a severe foot disease, he still didn't seek the Lord's help (2 Chronicles 16:12).

We don't know why. After all, this is the guy to whom the

Lord had said, "I'll be with you when you are with Me. And if you seek Me, you will find Me" (2 Chronicles 15:2, paraphrased). This is the king who had called on the Lord with these words when a million-man army came against Judah: "LORD, there is no one besides You to help in the battle between the powerful and those who have no strength; help us, LORD our God, for we trust in You, and in Your name have come against this multitude. LORD, You are our God" (2 Chronicles 14:11).

Asa's decision reminds me of an ultramarathon runner named Joasia Zakrzewski. At a 2023 race in England, she finished the 50-mile course, but she was disqualified after race technology revealed she had traveled almost 2.5 miles of it *by car*. (What gave her away was that she had covered one of those miles in one minute and 40 seconds—at racehorse speed.)

Like you, I don't want my obituary to read: "He followed God most of his life. He ran the race except for those few miles..."

Whatever was up with Asa, we can't let that be us. You finish what you started for God, and I will too. From beginning to end, we need His strong support.

Think About It: Make this version of 2 Timothy 4:7 your mantra: "I will fight the good fight, I will finish the race, I will keep the faith."

100

FAMOUS LAST WORDS

Behold, today I am going the way of all the earth, and you know in all your hearts and in all your souls that not one word of all the good words which the LORD your God spoke concerning you has failed; they all have been fulfilled for you.

JOSHUA 23:14

Joshua's legacy stands in contrast to Asa's because Joshua's devotion lasted a lifetime. We know this for a fact; we have his famous last words in Joshua 23–24 to all of Israel.

What this man of God—the successor to Moses, and Israel's leader for decades—said in his farewell address is worth repeating, because he lived it out so thoroughly. Let me share just a few excerpts from his powerful testimony about the God of Israel, the God Joshua served—the same God we serve:

> You have seen all that the LORD your God has done to all these nations because of you, for the LORD your God is He who has been fighting for you...Be very determined, then, to keep and do everything that is written in the Book of the Law of Moses, so that you will not turn aside from

> it to the right or to the left…You are to cling to the LORD your God, as you have done to this day. For the LORD has driven out great and mighty nations from before you; and as for you, no one has stood against you to this day. One of your men puts to flight a thousand, for the LORD your God is He who fights for you, just as He promised you. So take great care for yourselves that you love the LORD your God…Now, therefore, fear the LORD and serve Him in sincerity and truth… As for me and my house, we will serve the LORD (Joshua 23:3, 6, 8-11; 24:14-15).

Joshua is a shining example of someone who let God complete the good work He had begun in him so many years earlier (Philippians 1:6). Like the apostle Paul, Joshua "fought the good fight" and "remained faithful" (2 Timothy 4:7 NLT), all the way to his dying day. But here's the thing. As awesome as it is to give a farewell address, no Christian needs any famous last words as long as they have lived a faithful life. That kind of life speaks for itself.

Think About It: How you live should speak so loud, people can just point to your faithful life without saying a word.

NOTES

1. Charles R. Swindoll, *Come Before Winter…and Share My Hope* (Portland, OR: Multnomah, 1985), 134.
2. Swindoll, 135.
3. Ibid.
4. Jonathan Evans, *Fighting Your Battles: Every Christian's Playbook for Victory* (Eugene, OR: Harvest House, 2022), 218.
5. National Archives, Online Exhibit "Powers of Persuasion."
6. Matthew Poole, https://biblehub.com/commentaries/poole/1_samuel/17.htm.
7. John Piper, *Desiring God: Meditations of a Christian Hedonist*, rev. ed. (Portland, OR: Multnomah, 2011), 171.
8. Matthew Henry, "An Exposition, with Practical Observations, of the Book of the Prophet Hosea," verse 26, *Matthew Henry's Commentary on the Whole Bible, Vol. IV.—Hosea to Malachi* (MacLean, VA: MacDonald Publishing, n.d.), 1199.
9. Charles John Ellicott, "Commentary on Ephesians 3," *Ellicott's Commentary for English Readers*, verse 17, https://biblehub.com/commentaries/ellicott/ephesians/3.htm.
10. Ibid.
11. John Piper, "The War Within: Flesh Versus Spirit," desiringgod.org, June 19, 1983, https://www.desiringgod.org/messages/the-war-within-flesh-versus-spirit.
12. David Jeremiah, "Essentials of the Christian Faith: Spiritual Warfare Ephesians 6:12-18," *The Jeremiah Study Bible* (Brentwood, TN: Worthy Publishing, 2013), 1648.
13. Lewis Carroll, "To an invalid," *The Selected Letters of Lewis Carroll*, 2nd ed., ed. Morton N. Cohen (London: Palgrave Macmillan, 1989), 157
14. See Seth J. Gillihan, "How Often Do Your Worries Actually Come True?," psychologytoday.com, July 19, 2019, https://www.psychologytoday.com/us/blog/think-act-be/201907/how-often-do-your-worries-actually-come-true.
15. Interview with Susan Carnell, "U.S. Adults Report Increase in Binge-Watching During the Pandemic: Stress, Obesity and Associated Negative Binge-Watching Behaviors," *Clinical Connection E-Newsletter*, accessed May 7, 2024, https://clinicalconnection.hopkinsmedicine.org/index.cfm?objectid=662C6E80-583D-11EC-8929FE1F52376840.

BIBLE VERSIONS COPYRIGHT NOTIFICATIONS